D1560010

OUR SPIRITUAL RESOURCES

Books by JOEL S. GOLDSMITH

OUR SPIRITUAL RESOURCES

JOEL S. GOLDSMITH

Edited by Lorraine Sinkler

1817

Published in San Francisco by
HARPER & ROW, PUBLISHERS
New York, Hagerstown, San Francisco, London

Except the Lord build the house, they
labour in vain that build it.
—Psalm 127

Illumination dissolves all material ties and binds men
together with the golden chains of spiritual understanding; it acknowledges only the leadership of the
Christ; it has no ritual but the divine, impersonal,
universal Love, no other worship than the inner Flame
that is ever lit at the shrine of Spirit. This union
is the free state of spiritual brotherhood. The only
restraint is the discipline of Soul; therefore, we know
liberty without license; we are a united universe without physical limits, a divine service to God without
ceremony or creed. The illumined walk without fear
—by Grace.

—THE INFINITE WAY

OUR SPIRITUAL RESOURCES. Copyright © 1962 by Joel S.
Goldsmith. Copyright © 1978 by Emma A. Goldsmith. All
rights reserved. Printed in the United States of America. No
part of this book may be used or reproduced in any manner
whatsoever without written permission except in the case of
brief quotations embodied in critical articles and reviews. For
information address Harper & Row, Publishers, Inc., 10 East
53rd Street, New York, NY 10022. Published simultaneously
in Canada by Fitzhenry & Whiteside, Limited, Toronto.

Library of Congress Cataloging in Publication Data

Goldsmith, Joel S   1892-1964
          Our spiritual resources.

          Includes index.
          1. New Thought   I. Sinkler, Lorraine.
          II. Title
BF639.G5686   1978   289.9   78–16010
ISBN 0–06–063211–9

78   79   80   81   82   10   9   8   7   6   5   4   3   2   1

CONTENTS

PREFACE TO THE SECOND EDITION

Many persons have found it difficult to attain a balance between living by meditation and Grace and living effectively in the world, feeling that it is necessary to make a choice between one or the other. Since few persons are so situated that they can leave family or business responsibilities, they choose the world, hoping that someday they will be freed of these responsibilities and be able to devote themselves wholly to the spiritual life.

Our Spiritual Resources makes it clear that there is another way. Far from deterring us from entering upon the spiritual life, family, business, and social responsibilities can be a greater spur to spiritual unfoldment than retiring to a hermitage removed from the world. Of course, no one is ever totally removed from the world because even stone walls do not separate us from human consciousness. We are free of human consciousness only when it is dissolved through the activity of truth in individual consciousness.

Meeting everyday problems and responsibilities in the world, through the practice of spiritual principles, is a more effective way of attaining a realized fourth-dimensional consciousness of oneness than by withdrawing from the world. Problems and situations become opportunities for us to apply spiritual principles through meditation and practice. We thereby attain a realization of these principles, and mere intellectual knowledge gives way in us to a realized consciousness of truth.

The blending of deep spiritual wisdom with the practicalities of daily living, so characteristic of Joel Goldsmith's mystical teaching, shines forth from every page of *Our Spiritual Resources*, making it a textbook for living in the world without being of it. The light of spiritual wisdom is beamed upon practically every aspect of daily living. The pressures of life are relieved in the awareness that there is Something greater than human wisdom operating in individual experience when It is recognized and when, through meditation, a conscious contact is made with the Source of all good. The infinite capacity of the person who has touched the Center is released and life by Grace is attained.

Even though problems may still exist or come, the burdens drop away, and the seeker can now obey the scriptural injunction: "Come unto me, all ye that labour and are heavy laden, and I will give you rest. Take my yoke upon you and learn of me.... For my yoke is easy, and my burden is light" (Matt. 11:28–30). The burdens do become lighter as the yoke of oneness carries their weight.

The world we leave is the world of concepts. Even while living in the midst of its turmoil, heaviness, and conflict, we experience less and less reaction to it as we live out from that inner silence that quells all the noises of the world and is a "Peace, be still" to every problem.

To make this book more useful, an index prepared by Barbara Griffiths has been included in the new edition. An earlier version of the material in this book appeared in 1960 in *The Joel S. Goldsmith Letter*, a monthly message to Goldsmith students. The letters were then collected, revised, and published in 1962 under the appropriate title of *Our Spiritual Resources*, a book that has touched the lives of many persons and helped to awaken them to their potentialities.

—LORRAINE SINKLER

Palm Beach, Florida

CHAPTER I

THE NEW LIFE BY GRACE

This is the day which the Lord hath made; we will rejoice and be glad in it.   PSALM 118:24
Ye shall rejoice in all that ye put your hand unto, ye and your households.   DEUTERONOMY 12:7

G od is pouring Itself[1] forth and expressing Itself as harmonious being and as a harmonious universe. The world, however, is not enjoying the harmony of that universe or the harmony of God's being, but that is not because God is with-

Author's note: The material in *Our Spiritual Resources* first appeared in the form of letters sent to students of The Infinite Way throughout the world in the hope that they would aid in the revelation and unfoldment of the transcendental Consciousness through a deeper understanding of Scripture and the practice of meditation.

[1] In the spiritual literature of the world, the varying concepts of God are indicated by the use of such words as "Father," "Mother," "Soul," "Spirit," "Principle," "Love," and "Life." Therefore, in this book the author uses the pronouns "He" and "It," or "Himself" and "Itself," interchangeably in referring to God.

1

holding that harmony from anyone. There is no God that can be induced to do anything especially for you or for me, no God that will move out of Its orbit to do something for any one person that It is not at this very moment doing for everybody, whether or not all the everybodies avail themselves of what God is giving them so freely.

As you read this, review in your mind these questions: Do you believe that God is withholding anything from you? Do you believe that there is a God who can give you something, but at this particular moment is not giving it to you? Do you believe that? Is there anything that the hand of God is withholding from you? Is there any way that you can reach God to get God to loose something that you would like to have, and give it to you?

Most of the religious teachings of the world are based upon the belief that there is a way to influence God and thereby persuade God to act on our behalf. And now I ask you, do you believe that? Do you believe that you can find a way in which you can coerce God, influence or bribe Him with money, prayers, sacrifices, tithes, or with promises to be good? Do you believe that any of this influences God on your behalf? Do you believe that there is a way to open God's hand and make it let loose of the blessings which you think He is withholding from you?

Release yourself from the belief that there is a God withholding anything from anybody, anywhere, for any reason. God is not giving something to one race and withholding it from another or to one church and withholding it from another. There is no greater truth in all Scripture than that His rain falls alike on the just and the unjust. Once you begin to perceive that God is no respecter of persons, the inner release which comes from such recognition will break down any form of bias or bigotry—race prejudice, religious prejudice, economic or social prejudice—which you may have been entertaining.

You already know that the sun rises and sets on a schedule

that can be charted for hundreds of years in advance. The tides rise and fall on a set schedule; the seasons come and go on a set schedule; sun, moon, and stars move about in their orbits on a set schedule, without anybody's praying to God to bring it about, without anybody's trying to influence God. Do you know how much success anyone would have who prayed to God to interfere with the regularity of these natural phenomena? He would have no weight whatsoever with God, and all he could do in the end would be to destroy himself by his vain imaginings.

GOD'S GRACE OPERATES BECAUSE OF GOD, NOT BECAUSE OF MAN

Many a person has come to the latter years of his life, frustrated, defeated, and embittered because he has prayed for years, prayed for things that have not come to pass. Rather should every person release himself by conscious and persistent practice from any belief in a withholding God:

Here and now, I give up any attempt to influence God on my behalf, or on behalf of another. Here and now, I release myself and I release God.

Realizing that God's grace is omnipotent, omnipresent, and omniscient, I no longer look to God for anything or for anybody. God's function is to fulfill Itself, and inasmuch as nothing is by any means being withheld, nothing can by any means be given unto me.

God's grace is my sufficiency in all things. God's grace does not have to be won, earned, or deserved. God's grace is flowing as freely in the experience of this world as it is in the rising and setting of the sun, the ebb and flow of the tides, and the orderly movement of the planets.

God's grace is free and present everywhere. The place whereon I stand is holy ground because God's grace is here, and God's grace would be here even if I were the world's greatest sinner. My realization of this truth would immediately begin wiping out any sin and the penalties for such sin, none of which God has brought upon me, but all of which I have brought upon myself by living a life apart from this recognition of God's grace.

I relax and rest in the ever-present grace of God.[2]

A person in the deepest of sin, or a person at death's door with disease, or a person under a life sentence in prison can find his freedom, first by releasing within himself any desire that God do anything for him, by releasing God from any responsibility to do anything for him, and then by his acceptance of the fact that *God's grace operates because of God, not because of him.*

RELEASE GOD

Burning candles does not influence God. Sitting up all night in prayer does not influence God. This does not mean, however, that if we are led to light a candle or to sit up all night in prayer, we should not do so, because we should—not for the purpose of getting God to do something that God is not doing, but for the purpose of releasing ourselves from any doubt or fear that God is not here and now. There are times when it is necessary to sit up all night; there are times when it is necessary to work, to pray, to meditate, and to ponder for an hour or two, then rest, read a book, or take a nap, and then get up and begin all over again. "Pray without ceasing."[3] Work, work,

[2] The italicized portions of this book are spontaneous meditations which have come to the author during periods of uplifted consciousness and are not in any sense intended to be used as affirmations, denials, or formulas. They have been inserted in this book from time to time to serve as examples of the free flowing of the Spirit. As the reader practices the Presence, he, too, in his exalted moments, will receive ever-new and fresh inspiration as the outpouring of the Spirit.

[3] I Thessalonians 5:17.

work, watch and pray—not for the purpose of influencing God, but for the purpose of purifying ourselves of any belief that God is a withholding, a punishing, or an avenging God.

"God is love.[4] . . . God is light, and in him is no darkness at all"[5]—no punishment, no evil, no enmity. That is New Testament teaching. God is pure love, and that love is as tangible as the sun in the sky. As a matter of fact, the sun in the sky is a proof of God's love; the flow of the tides is a proof of God's love; the fact that papayas come from papaya trees, pineapples from pineapple bushes, and sugar from sugar cane—all this is a proof of God's love, a proof that there is a loving provision for the continuity of unfolding good. Every blade of grass on the green lawn testifies to the fact that God is love.

God is not a superhuman being; God does not think or feel as man does; God has no emotions such as man has. Sometimes when we read of acts of supreme cruelty on the part of human beings, our first reaction is, "I'd like to get my hands on that person"; or, "I wish he were only five foot five and I were six foot five, and we could meet!" That is a normal reaction, but God is not like that. God does not have the power to strike anyone down for his sins; God does not have the power to punish sins; God does not have the power to give or to withhold.

God is love; God is life, life eternal; and to know Him aright is life eternal. It makes no difference what our condition as a human being is when we begin to know Him aright. We can learn to know Him in the very depths of sin, disease, lack, limitation, or death; and when we do, we are lifted out of all such conditions, not because God has changed toward us, but by virtue of the fact that *we* have changed toward God. When we stop looking to God for something, that is when harmony begins to unfold in our experience.

[4] I John 4:8.   [5] I John 1:5.

An analogy to this relationship can be found in our human experience. Once we cease looking to a person for anything—for gratitude, payment, recognition, or commendation—usually it flows to us in abundant measure. We withhold it from ourselves by expecting it; and we set up a wall of defense in husband or wife, child, parent, or friend by the very act of expecting something from him or her, whereas if we were to set everyone completely free and expect our good from the one Source, we would then find that our husband, wife, child, parent, and neighbor would be bringing us their gifts with open hands.

The moment we look to anyone for favors or influence, we shut off our supply because the person from whom we are expecting something has an intuitive feeling, and whether or not he knows what we have in mind, he automatically sets up a wall of defense to protect himself from such attempts.

Let us release ourselves in this hour, and more than that, let us release God—release God from any obligation to us and recognize that God's only obligation is to maintain and sustain His own spiritual universe.

Set God free! God owes *us* nothing, but God owes *Himself* the joy of living freely and joyously—freely expressing, freely being—and we are the recipients of God's grace.

In true spiritual work, no demands are made upon one another, but everybody is set free to work out his own unfoldment in his own way. There are no "Thou shalt's," nor are there any "Thou shalt not's," and it is for this reason that we find such a deep spiritual bond among us. It is a bond that is built on love, and love does not bind.

We are all bound, however, by our own concepts of what we accept. We are even imprisoned in our religious concepts because these erroneous concepts of God limit us and hold us in bondage. Over and over again, I have emphasized that one of our major tasks is to understand the nature of God. Once we understand that, we can never ask God for anything, nor can we advise God about anything. Therefore, when we pray or meditate, it is not for the purpose of influencing God.

GOD IS FOREVER UTTERING HIS VOICE

Today, this very moment, carefully examine your attitude toward, and concepts of, God so that when you sit down to pray or meditate, you are not going to God for something: you are going within yourself, and, if you must think thoughts, then let them be along this line:

Thy grace is my sufficiency. Thou knowest my need even before I do, and it is Thy good pleasure to give me Thy kingdom. "Son, thou art ever with me, and all that I have is thine"[6]— is mine. All that God has is mine.

The very place whereon I stand is holy ground, because I and the Father are one. Where I am, God is; where God is, I am.

With just one or two or three minutes of such assurances, you are now ready for the experience of inner communion, because now you have nothing more to think. After you have assured or reassured yourself of all that God is, and opened your ears, you are ready for any impartation that God may have for you.

Does God ever have an impartation especially for you? No, God is no respecter of persons. The same message that you are to hear, anyone could hear provided he is tuned in to it. Tuning in to God is similar in a sense to tuning in to radio or television. There are not different programs for each home. There is just one program at a time going out from any one radio or TV station, and anyone who tunes in to that station can receive that particular message. In like manner, God is forever expressing God; God is forever expressing Himself; God is forever expressing truth; God is forever expressing life; God is forever expressing love; and when you tune in to God, you receive truth, life, or love, assurance or comfort. The particular

[6] Luke 15:31.

message that you receive is the one which your particular consciousness interprets for you in accordance with your need.

The voice of God is forever uttering Itself, and when He utters His voice, the earth melts. If we go to God in grief, the message that will come to us will interpret itself as comfort; if we go to God in lack, probably ravens will appear bringing food, or the birds will sit on our head, or fish will jump out of the sea into our boat, or somebody will come to our door with a basket full of food or dollar bills.

Whatever form it takes will merely be our interpretation of the word of God as it comes into our individual experience One person will tune in and find that a lump has disappeared, another that a fever has subsided, still another one that a stone has dissolved, and someone else that a bone has knit. God is not doing all those various things: God is uttering Itself as the healing Word. When we sit down in our meditation with a broken bone troubling us, it is a broken bone that gets healed, or if it is an upset stomach, that is healed; but do not believe that God is thinking in terms of us and an upset stomach or a broken bone, for that would be foolishness indeed and limitation.

Now let us continue this exercise in which we release ourselves from any concept of God as either a giving God or a withholding God, realizing:

God is! God's function is to be God, Good. God's activity is expressing Itself as life, truth, love, as the rhythmic flow of the grace of God, just as the tides are changing at this moment, as the sun is in motion at this moment, and the stars, and in this moment as the grass is growing. Sap in the center of the trees is rising and ultimately will come forth as fruit. That is all taking place in the now. Even though in the bitter cold of winter, we might look at the tree and behold it barren, yet within, God is fulfilling Itself, and in their due season, leaves, buds, blossoms, and fruit will appear—all by the grace of God.

GOD'S GRACE IS UNIVERSALLY OPERATIVE

We may look at our own lives, and they may at this moment be barren: there may be an absence of spirituality; there may be an absence of peace, happiness, joy, and contentment; there may be an absence of prosperity or health—all of which are states of barrenness. But at this very instant the years of the locusts are being restored. At this very instant, the kingdom of God within us is pouring Itself forth into expression, which in due time will be fruitage in our lives—*if* so be we are practicing this lesson of releasing God from any obligation to us, of releasing ourselves from any expectancy that God is going to single out either you or me to do something for us that is not already being done on our left hand and on our right hand:

I am satisfied that God is being God, and I ask nothing more than that. I release myself from expecting anything of a personal nature because I know that God's grace is my sufficiency, but not God's grace merely for me—God's grace, universally expressing, is my sufficiency. I acknowledge God in all my ways.

I acknowledge God to be my very life, the only law governing me, the only substance, and the all-supply. I acknowledge that this is a universal truth because, as I look down into the sea, I know the fish are being fed and that God has placed food in the bottom of the sea for all manner of fish. As I turn my gaze up into the air, I behold that the birds are fed and that wherever they turn there is food. God's grace has placed food in the sea and in the air, and the cattle on a thousand hills.

"The earth is the Lord's, and the fulness thereof."[7] And this earth is full—full of coal and oil, iron and gems—full, full, full. God's grace has filled this universe, and wherever travelers go, from east to west or from north to south, there is always fulfillment. Even in the frozen northland, there is food and clothing, because there is no place where God's grace is not flowing.

[7] Psalm 24:1.

I can never be outside God's grace while I understand the universality of His grace.

This wipes out for me all religious separation, racial or economic separation, for now I see that up above, on the earth, and down beneath the earth, God's grace is free. In the Orient as well as in the Occident, God's grace is abundant.

God is not withholding; therefore, God cannot give: God is forever in expression. And I shall live with that word is. *God is, Good is, Life is, Infinity is, Omnipotence is, Omnipresence is. My prayer is to know this truth, not to set forces in motion.*

Thy grace is fulfilling Itself, and that is enough for me to know. And since this Grace is universal, neither I nor anybody on earth is excluded from its operation. If there is any exclusion, then I am excluding myself, and that only because, in my ignorance of this great truth, I have been looking to God to give me or someone else something; I have been trying to influence God on my behalf or on behalf of someone else; I have not set God free as the infinite Intelligence and the divine Love of this universe. I do not even ask healing for Jones, Brown, or Smith, for I know that there is no healing to be withheld, and none to give. Thy healing grace is where I am, where he is, where she is—to be enjoyed, not entreated; to be accepted, not prayed for.

Thou all-knowing Wisdom, Thou divine Love, forgive me for having intruded in Thy province. I offer no advice; I make no suggestions; and I ask for no favors. Thy grace is my sufficiency in all things.

ABIDE IN THE CONSCIOUS REALIZATION OF OMNIPRESENCE

The very act of not recognizing Omnipresence sets up a sense of separation. The very act of entertaining mentally a desire for something sets up a separation from it. Nothing can take place in your experience except as an act of consciousness. Therefore, it is you who must daily have a period of meditation in which you can even take such an extreme stand as to ask

God to forgive you for the prayers of petition you have uttered in your life and for the things you have expected of God, ask God to forgive you for the disappointments and frustrations you have permitted yourself to feel by believing that God has not given you what was rightfully yours.

Free yourself and free God. Then open your consciousness to the realization, "Where God is, I am. All that the Father has is mine, and this is universally true."

God is not a power that can be invoked. You might remember that statement: *God is not a power that can be invoked.* God is a power, the power which created, maintains, and sustains this universe, but no one can invoke God's power, although we can sit in the silence and let God's power embrace us, permeate and fill us because it is Omnipresence. So to experience God's power is a matter of consciousness—whether or not we are consciously accepting it. But it cannot be invoked because it is never absent; it cannot be used because it is infinite; and therefore there is nothing and nobody on which to use it, for there is nothing separate and apart from that power.

The way to enjoy God's power is to sit in the silence:

Where Thou art, I am; where I am, Thou art—in a rubber boat on the ocean or lost in the desert, up in a plane or down in a submarine. Where I am, Thou art. My consciousness is filled with the living presence of Thee, almighty God. I cannot invoke Thy power; I cannot make it operative in my experience and I cannot stop its activity, but I can avail myself of its blessing by this acknowledgment.

There is the secret. Whatever comes into our experience has to come through our consciousness. If the power or the presence of God is to come into our experience, it has to come in by our consciously accepting it. "Ye shall know the truth, and the truth shall make you free."[8] Nowhere does Jesus indicate

---

[8] John 8:32.

that truth is not here, or that we must earn it or deserve it. What he says is that we must know it:

My consciousness is filled with the presence and power of God. God constitutes my consciousness. God is the substance of every fiber of my body and being, the very substance of my life. Even my body is the temple of the living God, because God is the very essence and law unto His creation.

By consciously knowing this truth, it becomes active in our experience. If we do not know this truth, it is as if we were cut off from it, and even though it is in our consciousness, it is not operative because we are not consciously embodying it.

This operates much the same as our Infinite Way work. The Infinite Way can prove to be a blessing to you only in proportion to your ability to embody its principles in your consciousness. That is why one goes only so far with it, and another one a little farther, and another one right to the end of the road. It is all in proportion to the individual's ability to know the principles and to abide by them and to let them abide in him.

If you abide in the conscious realization of Omnipresence and stop trying to get God to do something for you, you will come into the benefit of the God-presence and the God-power which is never separate or apart from you. It is never separate or apart from the drunkard; it is never separate or apart from the sensualist; it is never separate or apart from the beggar; it is never separate or apart from the vilest person or the sickest one. All that is lacking is recognition—acknowledgment.

The whole secret of Francis Thompson's poem, "The Hound of Heaven," is that he found God only when he stopped searching for Him. God was really hounding him to open his inner eye and his inner ear and become aware that God was closer to him than breathing, but he just kept running away from Him, until one day he fell unconscious in the street and then, when his thinking mind has ceased to function, God could come in and say, "Well, here *I*[9] am. *I* have caught up with you."

[9] Wherever "I" appears in italics, the reference is to God.

And that is what the world is doing. It is running away from an omnipresent God, which is attained, not by seeking It but by relaxing into It. Ask nothing of God because that sets up a belittling of God within yourself, as much as to say, "I know my need, but You, almighty God, do not, and so I will enlighten You."

We cannot enlighten God or invoke God, nor can we be worthy or deserving of God; we cannot entreat God, plead with God, or use God. God is closer to us than breathing; God's grace is our sufficiency, and, relaxing from all mental strain and striving, God will declare Itself to us, within us. And when It does, we discover that It was there all the time: "I will never leave thee, nor forsake thee.[10] . . . I am with you alway, even unto the end of the world.[11] . . . Whither thou goest, I will go . . . thy people shall be my people."[12] So it is that you will discover God once you release Him from all obligations to you, from all expectancy, and just realize:

I am satisfied that there is a sun in the sky, there is a moon, there are tides, crops and cattle, and that these are universally Your gift to Your beloved son, which I am—the very expression of God's own being, the very extension of God-consciousness as my individual consciousness.

In healing work, for yourself or for others, do not go to God as if you wanted God to do something for your patient or for your child or parent. That will not get you anywhere on the spiritual path. Go to God with the realization of God's presence, God's power, God's all-wisdom, God's good pleasure in giving you the kingdom; and when you have filled yourself with the assurance that God will never leave you nor forsake you, that God will be with you unto the end of the world, that even if you go through the valley of the shadow of death, God will go with you, then relax. That should be enough assurance for anybody to enable him to relax with no questions, no

[10] Hebrews 13:5.   [11] Matthew 28:20.   [12] Ruth 1:16.

doubts, or requests except, "Just let me sit here in Thy presence, in Thy peace."

BE WILLING TO RECEIVE GOD'S GRACE ON GOD'S LEVEL

As you learn to be still and receptive, there flows into you that moment of stillness, peace, grace, or release; and then as you go about your business, whatever demonstration is necessary on the human plane begins to come through. All healings are not instantaneous. Sometimes prayer must be continued over periods of days, weeks, and sometimes months. Occasionally, the reason may be that the practitioner is not sufficiently high in consciousness to bring through an instantaneous healing, but more often than not the reason is that the patient is not quite ready to receive God's grace on God's level, and is still entertaining some preconceived idea as to how the healing should come through. And God does not operate that way. The things of God are foolishness unto man, and the things of man are foolishness unto God. Very often, patients expect the healing to come about in some particular way or according to their preconceived notion of what is the right solution to the problem.

I remember a man who came to me many, many years ago to ask me to do some praying for him so that he could obtain work. When I asked him if he was sure that he wanted work, he replied that of course he wanted work since he had no employment.

"Well, suppose you get work and there is no salary attached, no earnings?"

"Oh, no, not that kind of work. It must be work with a salary."

"Then, supposing you got the salary without the work? Wouldn't that do?"

"Yes, that would be all right."

"Then it isn't really work you want. It's a salary."

"Yes, I guess that's right."

"But now, why salary? Wouldn't it do just as well if you inherited this money?"

"Yes, that would be all right, too."

By the time we had finished, work was all forgotten. So it is with us. We go to God, and we have an idea of exactly how the demonstration is to come through—a salary, a home, a family, or this and that, when possibly our good may be five thousand miles from here. Instead, we want it to take place right where we are, and preferably by tomorrow morning.

Our work is to lift us into that higher state of consciousness in which there is no disease, no unhappiness, no lack, and no limitation. Therefore, if the patient is centering his attention on watching to see if the disease is disappearing, he is likely to continue for several years before anything happens. When a seed is planted in the ground, the fruit does not appear the following morning. There are processes that must take place before the fruit comes through, and there is no way of evading or hurrying those processes. So it is with us. The patient and practitioner recognize that they are not to look to the body for results, but if they are watching for any change at all, it should be to observe what change of consciousness is taking place in the patient: Are his ideals becoming higher? Is his mode of living something of a more spiritual nature? What transformation is taking place?

We really are not healers of disease. I do not know how to heal disease and never did. With me, healing comes as the result of an inner, realized conviction of the universal nature of God as Love, Life, and Truth, and the fact that It is all here and now where I am. Through my meditation this is brought into conscious realization, and when that release or flow comes, the patient experiences the healing. I cannot understand it. I have only watched through thirty years and have seen that it happens—sometimes quickly, sometimes slowly, and in some few cases never at all, according to what we can see.

Life, however, does not end at the grave. Each one of us will some day pass from human sight; but the Life, which is your life and mine, that Life which is consciousness, is eternal. Before Abraham was, I existed, and therefore unto the end of the world do we exist. So birth was merely a coming into this plane of life from another, and what we call death is just leaving this plane of life for another. It may well be that many prayers we have prayed here are coming to fruition there, just as many of the prayers we have prayed in one year, we witness come to fruition in another year.

How many times have we had people come into our experience for help and found that five, eight, or ten years later, a change has come into their lives, a change that really should have, and could have, come that first year if they had only been ready for the experience!

Such was my experience. I suppose I could have had my spiritual illumination twelve years before I had it—but I was not ripe, and it took thirteen years of ripening before that first experience came, and many, many years more before later ripenings came. Nothing comes all at once. Some people believe that this work is some kind of magic and that tomorrow they will wake up in heaven. That has not been my experience. It is a long road, a very gradual, uphill climb with some backslidings, and then starting all over again up that hill.

So let us this moment go forward on that uphill climb by releasing God from any obligation that we may have felt God owed us, and let God's grace be our sufficiency.

ACROSS THE DESK[13]

I am sure that most students, in the early study of truth, have in mind primarily the overcoming of the discords and inharmonies in their human experience and the attainment of harmony in the form of good health, more abundant supply,

[13] ACROSS THE DESK is a regular feature of each monthly *Letter* and pinpoints and underscores certain principles of the Message which are especially timely.

happier relationships, and other satisfying human experiences. At that stage of unfoldment, it is not usually recognized that this is merely a desire to exchange the evils of human experience for the good in human experience. Nor is it apparent to most students that even if physical health and economic abundance are attained, they are still subject to the vicissitudes of the calendar and the weather and alternating periods of boom or depression, war or peace—in other words, they still remain "man, whose breath is in his nostrils."

Inevitably, it dawns in our consciousness that something is missing and that there must be something more than this volleying back and forth between good health and bad, between abundance and lack, between happiness and unhappiness, between peace and unrest. Sooner or later, it is brought to our attention that we are to seek the kingdom of God, the attainment of that mind which was also in Christ Jesus—the fourth-dimensional Consciousness. And so our search takes a different turn.

My own experience has taught me that one is either touched by the finger of God and, by His grace, is automatically lifted into Christ-consciousness, or that one attains the Crown by way of the Cross. Usually, there is a combination of both.

I have learned that to know the correct letter of truth, to study and practice it, develops the actual consciousness itself. Sometimes one may take the problem of supply and work with specific principles of supply, studying and practicing them, until "in such an hour as ye think not" the realization dawns, and from then on, supply is ours as a matter of Grace—without effort, without taking thought, without the sweat of our brow. Or, we may work faithfully and consistently with some principle of health, studying, learning, and putting the principle into practice, until again one day all of a sudden it happens, and we enter the very consciousness of health. Thereafter, we do not maintain our health by taking thought or by treatments, but we are maintained and sustained by the grace of God.

And so it is that in the area of human relationships—family, business, or public—again we find the specific, correct letter of truth, and we work faithfully with it, studying, remembering, consciously bearing witness, and putting into practice the specific principles, until a light flashes, an inner release comes, and then on that subject are we made free. Of what are we made free? Of the inharmonies and discords of ordinary human relationships—made free in spiritual relationship, the relationship of Christ, or spiritual being.

Students ordinarily believe that if they attain a flash of light or a momentary sense of God's presence, they are automatically freed from the entire round of human experiences, but my experience indicates that this is not true. Our release from what the Master called "this world" is gradual, piece by piece, until in a certain moment we are able to reach that point where we feel we are beginning to overcome the world in some small measure. But just as the Master attained his Crown through the Cross, so do we—it is not just one brief period of crucifixion, but a crucifixion of the physical sense of body, a crucifixion of the material sense of supply, a crucifixion of the human sense of relationships, bearing out the Master's statement that there is no wide and easy road to the attainment of the kingdom of God.

Students of The Infinite Way know that it will require diligent practice and faithful adherence to the principles of truth, and a sincere zeal in the application of them,[14] to attain the revelation of the fourth-dimensional, or Christ-consciousness. Symbolically, this is the attainment of Christmas, and our students must not be weary if they find, as I have found, that they must plod their way through the first arduous eleven months in order to attain the glory of the twelfth.

Now is come salvation, and strength, and the kingdom of our God, and the power of his Christ.

REVELATION 12:10

[14] These principles are clearly stated in the author's *Infinite Way Letters of 1959*, (London: L. N. Fowler and Co., Ltd., 1960), pp. 104-124, 169-225.

CHAPTER II

BEGIN PRAYER WITH THE WORD GOD

There is one principle of Infinite Way treatment which no student should ever forget: Never under any circumstances give a treatment to a person, a condition, or a disease. Never take a disease into a treatment; never take a condition into a treatment; never take a person into a treatment.

How is this possible? How can you avoid taking persons and diseases and sins into your treatment since every call for help that comes to you is from a person about a disease, a sin, or some kind of a condition? If you understand that a treatment is a statement of spiritual truth and that there is no truth about a person, a disease, or a sin, you will not find it too difficult to practice this principle because inasmuch as there is no truth about any of these there would be no possible way to give a treatment to a person, a condition, or a sin. The only truth there is, is about God, so the only thing you can ever treat is God.

Let me illustrate how this is done: Suppose that I receive a call from Mr. Jones who explains that he has bad digestion. Immediately, there is just one word that pops right into my thought—just one word. It would make no difference if the call were not from Mr. Jones, but instead was from Brown,

Smith, Blue, or Purple. Moreover, it would make no difference whether it were indigestion or polio, cancer, unemployment, or a contemplated divorce. There still is only one word that comes into my consciousness, and that word is God, G-o-d. No matter who the person is who calls and no matter what the nature of his claim may be—the house is burning down, the children have fallen into the lake—the answer is the same: one word—God.

Right in front of me is the word God. And what do I find as I look at that word? I find that God is infinite, therefore, ever-present; God is omnipotent, therefore, the only power; God is omniscient, therefore, the only wisdom and the only intelligence; and God is grace. If I were giving a treatment and it came to me that God is grace, the treatment would be all over at that moment, because such a flood of warmth goes through me when I contemplate God as Grace that it would spell the end of the problem, and that is what happens in a treatment when we keep our mind stayed on God.

Scripture says, "Thou wilt keep him in perfect peace, whose mind is stayed on thee." How else are we going to find peace? Have you ever thought about how difficult it is to find peace when you are thinking of the Joneses, the Browns, and the Smiths of the world? Have you ever found peace while you were thinking of sin and disease and death and poverty? Has anyone ever found peace while he was looking at the discords of the world? No, there is only one way to find peace. "Thou wilt keep him in perfect peace, whose mind is stayed on thee.[1] . . . Lean not unto thine own understanding. In all thy ways acknowledge him, and he shall direct thy paths.[2]"

Students frequently say, "I haven't enough understanding to heal," and I usually reply, "I haven't either, but I see a good many healings taking place." It is not your understanding that will ever heal anyone. "Lean not unto thine own understanding." Whether you are a practitioner, a teacher, or a beginner

[1] Isaiah 26:3.   [2] Proverbs 3:5, 6.

on the spiritual path, in every case that comes to you, lift your thought to God, acknowledge God's understanding and grace to be sufficient. Do you not see that no person's grace is your sufficiency and no person's understanding can help you? God's understanding, and God's understanding alone, is your freedom; God's wisdom is your guidance; God's love is your protection; God's presence is the harmony of your being. So with all your getting, get God. Forget about yourself; forget about your understanding; and hop right up there into God.

GIVE UP ALL ATTEMPTS TO DEFINE GOD

There was a time when God was a meaningless word to me —just a three-letter word, G-o-d, and those three letters did not spell a thing for me because I could not visualize God or understand what God meant. So, because I could not understand what God was, I preferred to use such terms as divine Mind, Principle, or Law. There are still many people in metaphysics who are in that same position today. But I found that after having gained some conception of God as Mind, Life, Soul, or Principle, I came back to the word God and realized that because it is a word that cannot be understood, it is the very best word of all.

Anybody who has a concept of God is praying to his concept: he is not praying to God. Anyone who thinks of God as Mind is thinking of an intelligence, probably a little superior to human intelligence, but nevertheless a kind of human intelligence. Anyone who is thinking of God as Love is thinking of love on some human plane. True, it may be pure like mother-love or father-love, sister- or brother-love, but nevertheless it is a human sense of love. The Love which is God is not that kind of love at all. God as Love has no relationship to anything that any human being can possibly think of as love; and so, until a person transcends all sense of human love, it is utterly impossible to understand God as Love.

Most of us are likely to entertain some idea as to what God

is, and then when we pray to that concept we wonder why our prayers are not answered. It is unwise to pray to any concept of God. It is far better to divest ourselves of all concepts of God. For example, in thinking and looking upon God as Love, we may turn to God and ask what Love is, and in acknowledging that it is not anything like mother-love, father-love, husband-love, wife-love, or child-love, nor anything like love for nature or love of beauty, finally we reach the place where we are willing to admit that we do not understand what love is on a God-level since we have never been God.

What is God as Mind? Quickly it comes that God is intelligence. Intelligence? How do we know that God is intelligence? What makes us call God "Intelligence"? To most people, intelligence is considered or thought of as cleverness, as knowledge, or as the capacity to act in certain ways under given conditions, but is God anything like that? What right does anyone have to limit God, and certainly if it is possible to know what intelligence is, that surely is limitation. No, we do not even know what God is as Mind.

God is Spirit, but what is Spirit? That we can never know. As a matter of fact, how can we really know anything about God since our knowledge must of necessity be finite? How can finite knowledge embrace the infinity and allness of God? Why not be honest and confess that we do not know what God is, and with that admission, we are really beginning to understand God because the minute we realize that we do not know or understand God, we are getting closer to It.

When we arrive at the place where we are absolutely stripped of every concept of God, of every belief about God or every theory about God, then we are drawing close to an actual God-experience. As long as there is any concept in our mind about God, it is finite, limited, and circumscribed, and therefore cannot be God Itself. We find God only when we drop our concepts and thoughts about God and are honest enough to admit, "There is only one thing that I can be sure of concerning God, and that is that God is. I do not know who or why or where God is; I only know that I have a feeling that there is a God." If we were to try to define God, we would fail because none of our definitions would satisfy us. We do not know why we know that God is; we just know.

When we reach the point where we acknowledge that God is, and when we are willing to stop there and not try to define *what* God is, we are at the most wonderful point in our experience for what we are virtually saying is, "Father, I know that Thou art. I know that there is a God. I know that there is Something beyond human selfhood, but that is all I know. Now, Father, reveal Thyself." At that moment, we are at the point of highest treatment or prayer. Our thoughts about God, our opinions and theories—all are dead, and we are a state of aliveness waiting for God to tell us what God is. In that state, God can reveal Itself. God can always reveal Itself to the expectant and receptive consciousness, the consciousness that is willing to annihilate its human wisdom, and in true humility acknowledge, "I know God is, but I do not know what God is or why God is, or where God is, or how God functions. I know not how to go out or how to come in."

Scripture says that we do not even know how to pray, but that we must let the Spirit bear intercession within us—let the Spirit pray. That is treatment as it is understood and taught in its highest form in The Infinite Way. I learned thirty years ago that it was absolutely impossible for me to know how to pray without trying to usurp God's place, but in the acknowledgment that all I know is that God is, gradually over the years there has come the conviction that if I turn to God and keep my mind stayed on God, the correct treatment, the correct prayer, the correct communion, the correct meditation, the correct way to heal, and the correct way to teach—all of these things—unfold from within.

For a long time to come it will not only be legitimate but essential in your treatment to know all the truth that you can possibly know, as long as you are knowing the truth about God and not about man—not about a person and not about a condition. Keep your mind stayed on God. The Browns, Joneses, and Smiths, the cancer and polio, will try to penetrate into your thought, but the ability to prevent their getting in is what makes you a practitioner. "What have I to do with thee—Jones, Brown, Smith, sin, disease, death? My work is with God. I shall keep my mind stayed on God—God, God, God."

GOD, THE ONLY ACTION

The claim may be abnormal bowel-action, but how can a bowel act any more than a heart, liver, or lungs? What good would it do to let your mind dwell on bowel-action, when you could not possibly make the bowels move, or the heart, liver, or lungs? All action is God-action, and God is the only action. You can only stay up here in God. Whether the claim is faulty digestion, whether it is bowels, paralysis, or mental infirmity, the treatment is the same:

God is the source of all action: God is the intelligence governing all action; God is the only action there is. There is no such thing as body-action in and of itself. Something has to operate upon the body in order to make it act. It is God that functions my being and my body, God that directs my mental and physical energies.

The claim presented to you may be one of unemployment. Would you attempt to take an unemployed person and give him employment? What guarantee would you have that he might not lose his job the next day or be placed in the wrong kind of a job? Instead of planning what should happen to this unemployed person, immediately turn to the word God:

God—God is infinite. Infinite? If God is infinite, God is the only. Then God is the only employer because there cannot be more than one. If God is infinite, that would include employee, too. God is both the employer and the employee, and the whole activity of employment, remuneration, reward, and recognition is taking place within God—God acting within Itself, God acting within Its own orbit, God acting within Its own being, God functioning Its own being.

Does that not mean that there are no human employers or employees? Does it not also mean that there are no periods of depression or recession? How can there be if God fills all time and space, if God is the only activity of being and the only law of being? If God is Spirit and if God is law and life, how can there be business or economic cycles?

GOD IS THE ONLY CREATOR

Always keep the treatment on the level of God. For example, what can you do about cases that come to you where married couples want children and have been informed by their physicians that for some reason or other they cannot have families? You can turn away from everything that is known about human generation:

There is only one Creator. God is the creative principle of this universe, and besides God there is no creative action, no creative principle, no creative substance—no creation at all except that which God creates.

God created the universe in the beginning, and if there is any creation of any nature, God is still the one and only creator of it. Actually, there is no creation: there is only evolving unfoldment. God is that out of which this universe, including individual identity, evolves. God is the source, God is the substance, and God is the activity of all being.

With the realization that man is not a creator, but that God is the only creator, in every case of this kind that has ever come to me, without a single exception, the couple has later had children.

The entire treatment always remains in God. It is true that in one case the claim presented to you may be one of inaction and in your treatment you may think of God as the source, seat, and activity of all that is. Another call may bring the claim of death or approaching death. Immediately, you might think of God as Life, the source and seed of individual life, the eternality, the immortality, the perpetuation, and the continuity of life. But always it is God, and you never come down to the level of man.

PRACTICE IS ESSENTIAL

As you keep your treatment on God, continue until something comes in spontaneously that completes the treatment, or until you come to the end of your treatment, that is, until you come to the place where you can think no more thoughts about God and are satisfied just to sit and wait and let God take over. If, however, you begin to be fidgety or mentally active and have not had your answer, stop the treatment, wait for an hour or two, and then go back and try it over again. Even then if you do not reach that point of satisfaction or completeness, get up and do it over again.

Do not hesitate to give ten, twenty, thirty, forty, or fifty treatments. You have nothing else to do from now until eternity except to find this conscious union with God, and if it is necessary for a few years to give ten, twenty, thirty, or forty treatments to every case, do it until you arrive at the place where automatically you can sit down, and God immediately takes over.

Everybody reaches that point through practice: nobody gets there without it. At first, there must be full and complete treatments, working with the idea of God from every angle, impersonalizing the error and *nothingizing* it, but then gradually as your consciousness is permeated with the Presence, your treatments take less and less time, until there are times when they do not take any time at all because the answer pops in as fast as the claims do.

You will find that most of the cases that come to you are easily and quickly met. Only about ten per cent of them give you real trouble, but with that ten per cent you really work. The compensation and the reward, however, are in those who respond more quickly, catch this light, and then eventually go out and do likewise.

Nothing has power but God, unless you make it so. Do not worry about your fears and do not worry about your sins. If you contact God, your fears and your sins will both disappear, and if you do not contact God, being pure will not help you. The purest men and women in the world have had horrible diseases and deaths. A person can be the most unregenerate sinner in the world, but he will be made as white as snow in the moment that he contacts God. It makes no difference what his fears or sins may be today. Do not sit in judgment on him; do not criticize or condemn him. Remember that your function is to reveal the Christ, and instead of sitting in judgment on the Magdalenes and thieves and alcoholics, turn around and love them, forgive them, understand them, and place them in God's keeping where God's love and God's forgiveness and God's grace can reach them.

One second of God-realization will dispel any sin, any disease, or any fear that has ever existed on the face of the earth—but it must be God-realization and not just talk about God or preaching about God. God-experience must come to you, and that experience is what dispels the sins, diseases, and illusions of the world. Keep your consciousness attuned to God, never bringing your thought down to the level of a patient, a discord, or an inharmony because, when you do that, your thought is not stayed on God, and you are missing the opportunity of experiencing God.

GOD IS THE LIFE OF INDIVIDUAL BEING

When you look at any person, you are not seeing the real person: you are seeing your concept of him, and there is nothing that you know about him that is true—not a thing. It makes

no difference whether you are seeing him with eyes of judgment, criticism, or condemnation, or, on the other hand, if
you are thinking of him as a paragon of virtue. In either case,
it is only a concept of him, and in either case it is wrong.
You might just as well not waste your time thinking evil about
him or thinking good about him, because in both cases you
are wrong, and in neither case are you bringing any healing
or health to him. Even when you are thinking the best about
him, you are not benefiting him. There is only one time when
you can be of help to a person, and that is when you can close
your eyes to the appearance and go straight to God:

*God is the soul of individual being; God is the life; God
is the only being. God governs, motivates, and animates individual being.*

Then you are giving a perfect treatment, then you are praying
for him, then you are upholding his hand; but the minute you
think of a person as being good or kind, you are not benefiting
him in any way whatsoever. You are "malpracticing" him because you are holding him in good humanhood. Good humanhood is only another form of humanhood, and sometimes the
good and the bad run into each other. The good becomes bad
one day, and the bad becomes good the next day. If you truly
want to bless a person, you will remember that God animates
and God permeates his being because God is the only true
being, the life and the soul of individual being.

Stop thinking of a person in treatment. Look over the head
of the person to where you can see neither a good concept
of him nor a bad concept, and realize:

*God is the only creative principle; therefore, God made all
people in His own image and likeness. God constitutes individual being. God loves his beloved child and God has been
with His child throughout all the ages. God has animated and
permeated the consciousness of His son and God fulfills Himself
as His son.*

*How wonderful are Thy ways, O God—not how wonderful
are you, O man. How wonderful are Thy ways, O Father, that
Thou maintainest man in Thy image and likeness. Thou art his
support; Thou upholdest his right hand; Thou it is who supports,
supplies, maintains, and sustains him.*

I never think of the Joneses or the Browns or the Smiths:
I think only how wonderful it is that God loves His children,
that God supports and upholds them, that God permeates
them, that God animates them, and that God is their true being,
so that there is no separation or division.

No sins of omission or commission can separate us from the
love of God, nor can any mistakes that we have ever made.
We live and move and have our being in God. We are studying
not to bring God into our experience or to find God, but to
have our eyes opened, to be awakened to the truth that now
already are we the sons of God.

Francis Thompson wrote:

> Does the fish soar to find the ocean,
> The eagle plunge to find the air—
> That we ask of the stars in motion
> If they have rumor of thee there?

Does the fish soar to find the ocean? No, the fish is in the
ocean. Does the eagle plunge to find the air? No, the eagle is
in the air. Do we study to find God? No, we are in God. Do
we meditate to find God? No, we are in God. Do we pray
to get God's grace? No, we are in God's grace. Do we have
anything in the world to do about our relationship to God
except to realize the Is-ness of it?

Now are we the sons of God and now are we living and
moving and having our being in God. Now God's grace upholds us. We study only because of a universal belief that we
are not in God's grace and are trying to get back into God.
But we have never left God—we have never left heaven. We
have always been in heaven, although we have accepted in our

minds a sense of separation from God. The truth is that we have never been, and can never be, separated from God: we have only accepted a sense of separation from God.

Our relationship with God is an individual one. It has nothing to do with anybody else in the world. Nobody can help it and nobody can hinder it. Therefore, in our daily meditation we must sit back and realize:

I and the Father are one; therefore, the identity of God is expressing as me, and the abundance of God is flowing through me.

Some people may find it difficult to accept this because they believe that their supply is dependent upon their business, their investments, or their inheritance; many women believe that their supply is dependent upon their husbands; practitioners, that their supply is dependent upon their patients; or teachers, that their supply is dependent upon their students. Your fulfillment is dependent not on any of those things, but on your conscious realization of your oneness with God. Within yourself, you have to release yourself:

God is my supply. My relationship with God constitutes my abundance, and it is because I am one with God that I have abundance—not because I am married, have patients, students, or a business. If I had none of these, still my relationship with God is: I and the Father are one, and all that the Father has is mine.

The harmony of my being is dependent only upon my realization of my oneness with God. The harmony of my body, the harmony of my purse, the harmony of my relationships in the world—all these are dependent not on what anybody else thinks or does. It does not even make any difference how many depressions there are, or how many wars.

My fulfillment is dependent only on my realization of my oneness with God. My oneness with God constitutes the harmony of my being. My oneness with God constitutes the fullness of my health, my wealth, and my supply. My conscious oneness with God gives me enough truth with which to meet every human need.

I am not dependent on person, place, or thing, nor can any person, place, or thing in the world affect my demonstration. My demonstration is the demonstration of my oneness with God, and that takes place within my own consciousness.

Here and now I dedicate myself to this truth: I and the Father are one, and all that the Father has is mine. God is the source of my being; God is the activity of my being. My relationship of oneness with God constitutes my harmony, and my oneness with God constitutes the allness and the all-harmony of my being, my body, my purse, and of my relationships.

I have everything in the realization that only God is my being. No one external to me can intrude in, or interfere with, my relationship with God. Oneness is my relationship with God and that conscious oneness nobody can take from me, nor can anybody add anything to me.

Because I love my neighbor as myself, I hereby know and declare that this truth is a universal truth; it is the truth about everyone on the face of the globe. I pray that God's grace will awaken everyone on earth to the infinity of his own being, so that no one on earth may ever again envy another, be jealous of another, or covet the possessions of another, whether individually, nationally, or internationally, since God's grace is his sufficiency.

From this moment on, I adopt as my way of life this statement: God's grace is my sufficiency in all things. No more do I look to man, woman, or child. No more do I argue or fight with man, woman, or child. God's grace is my sufficiency in all things, and henceforth and forever I look only to the Father for the infinity of my good.

ACROSS THE DESK

The mystical life is attained in one of two ways: The grace of God may touch an individual who has taken no thought about such an experience and who has not consciously prepared himself for the experience during this lifetime, or the grace of God may touch an individual and lead him to a spiritual teaching by means of which a process of *dying daily* begins, culminating in a rebirth into the Spirit.

In the first instance, as in the case of Saul of Tarsus who became St. Paul in one blinding flash, the introduction into mysticism compels the students to remain away from public life, until such time as spiritual maturity has taken place and he is prepared from within for some specific ministry and is then given the instructions, care, protection, wisdom, and all that is necessary for the fulfilling of the mission. In the early years of this ministry and the years preceding it, there are difficult times for the individual because the transition from "this world" to "My kingdom" is a difficult one.

To those who come by the second way, there are still difficulties because one cannot add new wine to old bottles, nor add new patches to old clothing, nor can one fill a vessel already full, and therefore the years of emptying out previous conceptions and many misconceptions prove difficult.

Then, to all on the spiritual path, comes the problem of making the transition from good health and abundant supply to physical well-being, or from material lack to material abundance, but this is only a way station on the path of The Infinite to physical well-being, or from material lack to material abundance, but this is only a way station on the path of The Infinite Way because our demonstration is not complete until we have risen above both the evil and the good of human experience.

As I look forward, I feel led to remind you of three revelations of The Infinite Way which should be continually receiving your attention:

Number one: The Infinite Way revelation of the nature of God. You will find that it requires many hours of many days and many months before you can rid yourself of the concepts that have been built up in human consciousness over these last thousands of years. It will not be easy to root out of your thought the belief that God rewards and God punishes, or that God can be influenced by man, or that one can go on being an ordinary human being and at the same time be the child of God who lives under the grace of God and to whom none of the snares or pitfalls come nigh.

It will be difficult at first to make your adjustment to the fact that you have to make your consciousness a fit dwelling place for the grace of God, and that you do not bring God down to yourself, but that you make yourself receptive to the ever-present God. It is not necessary to make God change toward you. In fact, that is impossible, but it is absolutely necessary that you change yourself to make yourself a fitting transparency for God. The way to accomplish this comprises approximately one-third of all Infinite Way literature.

Number two: All the centuries of human life have been based on seeking greater powers with which to destroy lesser powers, and even going to the extreme of seeking a God-power with which to overcome earthly powers. The Infinite Way revelation as to the nature of error, or evil of any kind, provides us with the missing link, so that we can know not only why the world with its wars, famines, tornadoes, tidal waves, epidemics, and other disasters has failed to experience God-power, but also the wisdom which results in the dissolution of these appearances which are based primarily on the universal belief in two powers.

Number three: Since God does not work through human consciousness as such, it becomes necessary that our individual consciousness be transformed so that there remains less and less of human consciousness as we attain more and more of the qualities of God. The hours spent in study and in the assimilation of what is studied, the hours spent in meditation and in practicing these principles result in the attainment of spiritual consciousness in which we come step by step to the surrender of the material sense of good as well as the material sense of evil, all of which constitutes "this world," and to the attainment of "My kingdom," which is the fourth-dimensional consciousness.

There is a spiritual Presence behind the activity of The Infinite Way. In fact, it would be better stated that there is a divine Presence which constitutes the activity of The Infinite Way and is responsible for its healing works, for its comforting, supporting, and supplying activity. It is this Presence which lives my life. This, however, is only important to you in proportion as you realize that God is no respecter of persons and that this is the same Presence that lives your life as you let yourself be governed by Grace rather than by taking thought or living by might or by power. The consciousness which constitutes my being constitutes your being, and it is only necessary for you to relax in the Word and rest in that Word.

Please keep ever before your thought that the goal is the attainment by you of spiritual consciousness, and that only in the enriching and the deepening of your own consciousness will it be possible for you to bring forth the spiritual fruitage of harmony in your own experience and in the experience of those who are led to you. You can be a blessing to those of your world and to those of the world at large only in proportion as your own consciousness is enriched and deepened by spiritual awarness. Out of the spiritualized individual consciousness come the great works of the masters, and in proportion to this deepening and enriching of consciousness will come forth the great works given you to do.

I do not expect that the day will ever come when there will be one church on earth, since for many generations to come there will be varying states and stages of consciousness, but this need not in any way interfere with the ultimate realization of the great truth that there is but one God, and this God is the God of all churches, and therefore, regardless of our affiliation or nonaffiliation, we are brothers to one another.

And now a final word: If you find it difficult to forgive those who have offended you or yours, pray daily that God forgive them. Forgiveness is one of the great spiritual qualities, but personal sense does make it difficult at times for us to understand and demonstrate the true nature of forgiveness. Nevertheless, we can always turn to God and ask that God forgive our enemies and awaken them in spiritual wisdom.

CHAPTER III

THE PRACTICALITY OF
SPIRITUAL LIVING

That the spiritual life is eminently practical is evidenced by innumerable episodes related in Scripture. For example, there were three Hebrews placed in a fiery furnace, and yet we are told that they came out without even the smell of smoke upon them, but it is also said that some saw a fourth man walking with them through the flames. The Gospels tell how Jesus was crucified and sealed in a tomb, yet those of spiritual vision later beheld him walking the earth. Saul of Tarsus, a persecutor of the Christians, was on his way to Damascus to persecute more Christians when he had the experience of beholding the Christ, of actually hearing the Voice. That transcendental experience made him a disciple of the Christian teaching, made him a healer, teacher, preacher, and the founder of churches; it had a very practical effect upon his life, but first, before that practicality could be demonstrated, he had to have spiritual vision.

In the material sense of life, we have built our individual affairs on the idea of achieving, accomplishing, and acquiring. In fact, the entire history of human existence is one of acquisition, fighting, and even stealing, or in some other way striving to attain material good, and yet this materialistic and apparently very practical approach to life has never solved the problem of existence for anyone. There are people who have acquired millions and multimillions, but rarely have they achieved happiness, contentment, or peace; and there are others with perfect physical health, but seldom do we hear that they have found peace of mind, peace of soul, or peace in human relationships.

Human experience stresses the wisdom of placing our dependence on things and persons to such an extent that we tend to feel secure when we have an adequate amount of dollar bills or to feel confident when the heart beats regularly, when the liver, the lungs, and the entire human organism are functioning perfectly according to human standards, and when everything in this outer world presents an appearance of harmonious activity in abundant measure. But such a standard of values is subject to the fluctuations of time and chance, and trouble arises the minute anything happens in that outer universe so that the desired number of dollars begins to disappear, the organs or functions no longer operate harmoniously, or discord in human relationships flares up, because the human mind has no way out of its predicament except to seek for more dollars or for an improved condition of the organism or for more satisfactory relationships with the same or with different people, and all too often it fails to find any solution to these problems.

The spiritual life is a complete reversal of all this. In that life, concern is no longer primarily for such material and worldly satisfactions, nor does our dependence rest on persons and things in the outer world. This, however, does not imply a negative approach to life, because the spiritual life is not a negation of anything or of anybody; it is not turning away from the practicality of dollars, the comfort of a healthy physical apparatus, or the joy of friendships. The spiritual life is not such an austere one that it denies the living of a normal life to anyone.

THE ACTIVITY OF GOD TRANSLATES ITSELF IN
TERMS OF DAILY EXPERIENCE

When we adopt the spiritual way of life, we first have to give up the more or less universal belief that as students of spiritual wisdom, relying on the things of the Spirit, we are not practical, and therefore we should not be interested in having good homes, good clothing, or good food. In some circles, there is a belief prevalent that spiritual integrity or progress in spiritual affairs in some way or other entails a lack of financial success or progress and often results in an actual lack of worldly goods, but nowhere in Scripture can one find authority for the blessedness of lack or limitation. True, Scripture does teach that the love of money is the root of all evil, but it says nothing about money itself being evil—only the love of it. It is all a matter of where one's dependence or faith rests.

Saul of Tarsus became St. Paul when he realized that the so-called intangibles, which the rest of the world did not see or hear, were the very substance of his outer experience. It was that which provided him with even such practical things as money. In city after city, many of the churches he founded were unable to finance themselves and, after a short while and in some cases a longer while, in their financial straits, they had to appeal to brother Paul for assistance. It was Paul, the preacher, the man of the Spirit, he whom the world today would call impractical, a visionary and a dreamer, who provided funds for the churches when the very practical members of their congregation were unable to do this.

The truth of the matter is that there is nothing more practical, progressive, or prosperous than a life lived in accordance with the Spirit. For example, the person imbued with the Spirit becomes a better businessman than the one depending wholly on his education or mental ability, just as the person imbued with God is a better musician or artist.

Great music is recognized almost universally as a product of the Soul, and even though there are musicians who play and sing perfectly, there is often no soul in their music. Not only is this true of music, but it is also true of building bridges or drilling for oil. There must always be a soul if the work is to attain the height not only of its beauty, but of its practicality. When Spirit is the animating and motivating force, then every activity of daily experience improves in quality as well as in quantity.

Unless this is clear to you, you will tend to separate your spiritual life from your practical or daily life and thereby defeat your purpose. Let us be honest. Most of us turn to God because of a sense of dissatisfaction or incompleteness in some area of our present life. It is the frustrations, the discouragements, and the disappointments that drive us forward because if we had a sense of completeness or perfection, if we had a sense of all good, there would be no incentive for further search. So let us accept this drive toward God, toward the Soul of man, as a drive to find self-completeness, satisfaction, and opportunity for progressive unfoldment.

THE INVISIBLE IS THE SUBSTANCE OF ALL FORM

In the opening passage of his great book, John speaks of God as the Word and of the Word becoming flesh and dwelling among us. My entire experience has been one of beholding God, the Spirit, become flesh—harmonious, healthful flesh—and that not only as the flesh of the body, but as the flesh of the pocketbook and the flesh of the everyday relationships with human beings in the world.

In the world of the Spirit, all financing can be done without recourse to human means. It is never necessary to ask anybody for money; it is never necessary to tell anyone our needs: we need only become quiet within our own being in the realization that the Truth in us, operating through the mind, is the substance of what appears outwardly, because mind forms itself as the dollars, as the seat in the airplane, or as whatever the need may be.

All limitation of whatever nature must be recognized as the carnal mind, which is made up of the belief in two powers, but which actually is not a mind since there is only one mind. This carnal mind has no law to maintain it and is not God-ordained or God-sustained. Therefore, in dealing with any problem of limitation, first recognize it as the carnal mind which is not a power, but a nothingness, the "arm of flesh"; and then, as you contact the Father within, realize your oneness with the Spirit, and feel that answering "click," you are at-one with your opportunity—with your position, with any capital neces-sary with which to carry on your business, or for that matter with help of any kind, human or mechanical.

If you needed a piece of machinery and if that piece of machinery were three thousand miles away, as soon as you recognized limitation as impersonal carnal mind, always with-out power and presence, and after you made your contact with God, it would be on its way to you. If you needed a book, and if it were at the other end of the world, as soon as you recog-nized lack in any form as impersonal error and after you made your God-contact, that book would find its way to you. It is a recognition that whatever is needed is to be found within your own consciousness, not somewhere external to it, and it appears when the need is felt because it has been embodied in your consciousness since the beginning of time.

That which is already your eternal demonstration is revealed through your contact with the Father within. Make your con-tact with the Father—in all your ways make the contact, whether the need seems to be for person, place, thing, circumstance, or condition, and then the day will come when you will not con-sciously have to make a new contact eight or nine times a day: the contact you have made will have become a permanent one.

Thereby, you make a transition from the material sense of life which claims that security is based on the amount of dollars you have and that you must use human means to acquire them, or from that material sense of life which places dependence in a pill or a plaster to that place in consciousness which recognizes that the Invisible is the substance of all form and appears outwardly as the necessary form, and that therefore, it is of the utmost practicality to turn within to the Source of that which is to appear without.

The real substance of all form is invisible. The world that appears is not made of anything that appears, but of that which is invisible. When a seed is placed in the ground, there is a life force which acts upon it, and that life force is invisible, but that life force invisibly acting upon the seed and the soil later appears as blossoms, flowers, and fruit. The visible is the result of an invisible Presence and Power. In horticulture, this Force is called nature, but by whatever name it is called, it is God, an invisible, infinite force and power which also is a law. That law is invisible, but the result of its action becomes visible and tangible as trees, blossoms, and fruit.

There is within you an invisible law in operation, which can be applied to your business, your home, your marketing, and to your financial situation. All outer effects are the product of the activity of that inner law, and all that comes into your outer experience you attract to yourself.

When you attract evil, it is because you have opened yourself negatively instead of positively. In other words, if you sit back in the attitude that anything can happen to you and a lot of things are likely to, you are opening yourself to a negative sense of the law. When, on the other hand, you recognize the nature of I and realize that the first chapter of Genesis gives you dominion, God-given dominion, over all that is, then you have positive laws at work in your experience.

SET EVERYONE FREE

Isaiah tells us to "cease ye from man, whose breath is in his nostrils: for wherein is he to be accounted of?"[1] And then

[1] Isaiah 2:22.

in the Psalms we are told, "Put not your trust in princes, nor in the son of man, in whom there is no help.[2] . . . When my father and my mother forsake me, then the Lord will take me up."[3] There is no human circumstance that can arise in your experience that will prove to be of any permanent destruction or harm or even of any serious inconvenience to you, *if only you will recognize that your dependence is not on father, mother, child, husband, or wife; but that your dependence is on the Infinite Invisible*. When you have come to the point of reliance on the Infinite Invisible, then you discover the law of harmonious relationships and learn how beautiful life can be.

Most of the discords in this world come from believing that we need something from someone, and each one is afraid that the other is going to take it away from him. There is a gnawing fear that we are not going to get our just dues or just desserts —sometimes, perhaps, a fear that we *are* going to get them. There is a fear that too much may be expected of us or that too little is coming to us. On the other hand, can you picture the joyful experience of going through life being friends with anybody and everybody in the whole world, knowing that no one has anything you need or want and you have nothing anyone else needs or wants, that all you require unfolds to you from within your own being? That makes sharing a double delight because it is a heartwarming experience to share with those who do not expect it of you or feel that you are under any obligation to them.

There is no room in spiritual living or in a spiritual activity for selfishness. The law of God is a law of love and cannot be utilized for selfish purposes. Love is one of the great attributes of God and must be expressed in our daily experience if we are to live in accordance with God's law. We are expressing love in proportion as we release the world of men and women from every form of bondage. When we hold an individual responsible for his sins, we hold him in bondage; but when we loose him and let him go in forgiveness, if necessary in the

[2] Psalm 146:3.   [3] Psalm 27:10.

realization that he knows not what he is doing, we are fulfilling the law of love.

There are those in our experience who humanly owe us an obligation, and we express our love by inwardly releasing them from that obligation, *but love does not mean that human obligations can be ignored or responsibility shirked with impunity.* In fact, sometimes the highest form of love is to require someone to fulfill his responsibility, thereby helping him to fulfill the law of love and giving him an opportunity to grow and live according to the high ethical standards the spiritual life demands. That does not mean, however, that spiritually we hold him in bondage to his debt or obligation, or in any sense are tempted to believe that our own demonstration can ever be affected by the attitude or actions of anyone else.

For example, according to all standards of business ethics, partners have obligations to one another, but spiritually, inwardly, each should release the other in the sense of mutuality, recognizing that a partnership is a reciprocal relationship based on intelligence and love. The fulfillment of that relationship is not from one partner to another, but from God to each one of them.

In every human relationship, "loose him, and let him go"[4]; *inwardly* release the individuals concerned from their human obligations in your experience. Your trust, faith, and confidence should always rest in God, not in man. Accept the principle that your good is the gift of God by Grace, and that the substance of your good is already intact, infinite, and complete within your own being and will unfold from within you.

Your good may still come through some other person or through some normal business transaction, but you are not depending on it to come from that direction, you are not outlining how it should come, nor are you holding someone in bondage to an obligation, hoping that if he fulfills his

[4] John 11:44.

responsibility your needs will be met. Rather, you are looking to the Father within who knows your need and whose good pleasure it is to provide for it. Inwardly, release the world of men and women from bondage and obligation so that you may find your oneness and completeness and wholeness in, and through, your God-relationship, and then you will find your self-completeness and perfection.

WORK, BUT WITHOUT STRUGGLE

The Christ operates freely in proportion to the relaxing of our personal efforts. For example, if I wanted to compose music or write a book or a play, I could best bring the activity of the Christ into my experience, first, by consciously realizing for a few moments that the substance of this new form is already within my own being, that it is mine as the gift of God, and then, by becoming very still, very quiet, and very peaceful in the assurance that this idea will become flesh in the form of notes or words, and thereby, become tangible in my experience. As I am able to cease from all effort, quite suddenly this new idea bursts upon me and unfolds. Whatever it may be—a new plot for a story, a new piece of music, a new poem, a new design for a home—it will come by Grace. Our good is not to be earned by the sweat of our brow; it is not to be labored for: it is to come to us gently, peaceably—by Grace.

This does not mean that we will not work hard. On the contrary, we shall be working harder than ever before because we shall be given so much more work to do; but that work will not be in the nature of struggling for success—fighting for ideas, competing for partners, for financing, or for recognition or reward. All that will be done for us as we learn to relax in the Spirit. There is Something that will carry us through every experience, and that Something is now alive, alert, and awakened in our experience.

Rest more, relax more, realize more and more that it is the

Invisible which appears visibly. Whatever appears as outward form is but the result of your own inner Grace, and that inner Grace which has been given to you is appearing and always will appear every moment of every day in the visible and tangible form necessary to your abundant experience.

In order that you do not at any time accept the belief that you have the right to outline to this Spirit within what the nature of your demonstration is to be, always be sure in your meditation that your attitude is one of realizing that God is infinite intelligence, that God knows the nature of the demonstration, and that you are receptive to whatever form the demonstration is to take.

During the last year of my business experience, my business had become very bad; and every day, instead of becoming better, it grew worse, even though all the while I was having treatments for better business, by which I meant more orders and more profits. The more the practitioners worked for me, however, the worse my business became, until finally there was no business at all. Three times in one week I was told that I had no right to be in business, but that I should be in the practice of spiritual healing. That was something of which I had never dreamed, but after being told for the third time that I should be in the practice, I opened an office as practitioner, and then all those treatments and prayers began to bear fruit—not in more orders, but in patients and expressions of gratitude. The situation was met, but not in the way that I had thought it should be.

Very often we are inclined to outline just what our demonstration is to be, whereas the wisest course is to take the attitude of receptivity and let the Spirit inform and direct us in the way in which we should go. Then, if we follow that way, we shall find our footsteps prospered from every standpoint and from every angle. It is when we go contrary to the leading of the Spirit that we encounter all manner of human obstacles.

FULFILLMENT IS WITHIN YOUR CONSCIOUSNESS

Infinite good is already established within your own consciousness. Therefore, you cannot add good to yourself, but through persistent practice you can learn to let good flow out from within your own being. God is the law operating in and as your own consciousness, and because God is infinite, your consciousness is infinite. Therefore, your consciousness is all-inclusive and this very moment includes the substance of everything necessary to your experience unto eternity—if you live seven billion years, which you will. The substance of all that is necessary for your unfoldment is at this very moment embodied within you.

This will clarify itself for you if you think of the work of a structural engineer engaged in the building of bridges. The idea for the bridge is already within him, and all he is called upon to do is to bring it forth into form on the drafting board. Every idea necessary for the completion of that bridge—or for that matter for a piece of music, a poem, or a plan for a house—is within individual being, and as a person learns to develop that listening ear and that inner vision, it will pour itself out for him on paper. Moreover, not only will the idea take form, but if it must be financed, money will pour itself out for that purpose, too.

In other words, the substance of everything necessary to your experience is already within your own being and ready to unfold naturally as it becomes necessary to you, because the completeness and perfection of your life is already established within you as essence or substance and it appears outwardly as form. Your part is to learn to sit in your quiet moments of meditation, realizing this completeness and understanding that the only barrier to the expression of perfection is the belief in two powers, which constitutes the carnal mind, but which must be recognized as no power since there is only one power, God.

Relax in the awareness that within you is the fulfillment of life, and with this recognition the flow begins. The Master promised, "I am come that they might have life, and that they might have it more abundantly."[5] *I* am come, that *I* within you is come that you might be fulfilled.

Fulfill yourself as parents; fulfill yourself as housekeepers; fulfill yourself as children of God; fulfill yourself in harmonious, abundant, and progressively good experiences. That *I* within you is there for that purpose, and your meditation is a relaxing in the realization that the carnal mind is not power and that the Infinite Invisible, which is the invisible Substance of your being, the invisible Consciousness, and the invisible Soul of you, is the essence of all form. It is your Saviour and your protection in your every daily experience.

When the mental and physical struggle for the good things of life is given up, all good begins to unfold naturally and without effort. This is living by Grace; this is following Jesus' teaching which is the foundation of the entire message of The Infinite Way: "Take no thought for your life, what ye shall eat, or what ye shall drink; nor yet for your body, what ye shall put on. . . . Your heavenly Father knoweth that ye have need of all these things.[6] . . . for it is your Father's good pleasure to give you the kingdom."[7] The nations of the world struggle after things, fight for things, go to war for them, and even pray for them, while all the time their heavenly Father knows that they have need of these things, and it is His good pleasure to give them the kingdom.

The life of the Spirit is a relaxing in the realization that the essence, or substance, of all good is already within you and is unfolding in your experience in an orderly, progressive, and abundant fashion. That is the new life by Grace in which the Christ is alive and active in your consciousness, and from then on it will be impossible for you to avoid experiencing the

[5] John 10:10.   [6] Matthew 6:25, 32.   [7] Luke 12:32.

fruitage of the Christ, *but in what measure will depend upon you.* The principle is clearly stated, and therefore, the degree or amount of fruitage experienced rests with you individually.

The Infinite Way is like unto "My kingdom," which the Master tells us, "is not of this world," and the function of The Infinite Way is not to give us merely the peace that "this world giveth," but a deeper, more enduring peace. From a practical standpoint, this means that while we do not concern ourselves primarily with curing diseased bodies or increasing the amount of our dollars, nevertheless, as this "*My* kingdom" and "*My* peace" are attained, health of mind, body, and supply are the inevitable "added things."

The goal of our attainment is spiritual awareness. Our writings and recordings reveal the principles of spiritual living, which when practiced deepen and enrich consciousness. This *attained consciousness* is the Christ which now lives our lives, becomes our bread, meat, wine, and water, becomes the resurrection from the tomb of material living, raising us to the life of divine sonship so that we no longer live "by might, nor by power," but as an heir of God.

In healing work, remember that we cannot meet a problem on the level of the problem; that is, we cannot attain health by overcoming disease; we cannot have abundance by increasing our supply of dollars; we cannot attain companionship by friendships or marriage. Only by turning thought *from the appearance* to the realization of God as Omnipresence and Omnipotence and attaining the actual experience or awareness of the Infinite Invisible, do we find the harmonies of life appearing consistently and abundantly. The visible evidence may well be the health of mind and body, the abundance of supply, and satisfying friendships or marriage. These come as the *fruitage* of the attained consciousness of God. In *Living the*

Infinite Way[8], there is a chapter, "God Is Omnipresent," which deals more fully with this subject.

Our study and practice will assuredly reveal a full and rich life, complete with the added things when our desire for things has given way to the desire to know God, whom to know aright is life eternal.

[8] Joel S. Goldsmith (New York: Harper & Brothers, 1961), pp. 99-115.

CHAPTER IV

TRANSITION

Those who are on the spiritual path do not die: they make a transition which is in no way related to what the world calls "dying," because this transition is not an act of their own: it is an act of God and takes place by the grace of God. If you will look back on your own experience, you will gain a better understanding of this whole subject. You came into this world as an infant, and when you made the transition from infancy to childhood with an entirely different looking body, you did not die or pass on: you simply made a transition.

Some years after that, you reached the age of puberty, and another change took place in your body, but it was not dying or passing on: it was merely a transitional stage into another phase of life. Then, as you reached your upper teens, you passed into still another phase of life, completely different from the twelve-, thirteen-, or fourteen-year stage. All of life took on a different complexion because you had made a transition out of childhood. Dolls and toys no longer interested you, and even basketball, baseball, and football ceased to be the center of your world because the world outside the playground and the neighborhood movie stretched forth in ever-widening horizons.

So you continued until one day you found yourself in truth, and when you became a serious truth-student, you found yourself in another world, a world in which bridge, golf, dancing, and the theater occupied a minor place in your life, and, in some cases, were left behind completely because now in this new life your attention was focused on God. It was a transition from "this world," the world to which Jesus referred when he said, "I have overcome the world."[1]

There was no death about that transition, except a death to materiality or what Paul called "dying daily," dying daily to old modes of thought and reliances. There was a time in our experience when our primary concern was that we have a normal heart and normal blood pressure. We relied on food, climate, or diet, whereas now our only reliance is on our realization of God. It is a complete transition out of "this world" into a new world, a new state of consciousness, which has rightly been called the fourth dimension of life in which we live very nearly a completely spiritual existence and in which dependence is not placed on anything or anybody in the external world.

And so we go on from transition to transition until one day —we do not do it, but it is done for us—we pass from sight, and undoubtedly, as far as the rest of the world is concerned, we shall leave a body to be buried or cremated. That also is part of the illusory sense of human existence; but there will be no body there because we carry our body with us wherever we go.

ONLY THE SPIRITUALLY ILLUMINED RECEIVE
THE SIGN OF IMMORTALITY

When Pilate reminded Jesus that he had power to crucify him or to set him free, Jesus answered, "Thou couldest have no power at all against me, except it were given thee from above."[2] Pilate had no power to take from Jesus his life, and, as a matter of fact, he probably would not have had power

[1] John 16:33.   [2] John 19:11.

to crucify him, had Jesus not been willing to submit to it. Submitting to the Crucifixion was Jesus' way of proving to the world that he could lay down his life and that he could pick it up again, thereby demonstrating not only that Pilate had no power to take the life of Jesus, but that no temporal power—no sin, disease, bullets, or bombs—has the power to take the life of any man.

In this age, we do not voluntarily submit to being shot, crucified, or bombed, but we do know that if for any reason we should be subjected to such experiences, our lives would not be at stake because there is no temporal power that can destroy Life. Few there are in today's world, however, who would not take violent exception to this, because the world at large puts its faith and trust only in what it can comprehend and grasp by means of the five physical senses. Little else is ever given credence.

This was equally true in the very first days of the Christian era when only the spiritually illumined saw Jesus after the Resurrection. Those immersed in materiality were unable to see him after his burial because they had not risen to that height of spiritual apprehension. Never forget that it is only the spiritually illumined who are given irrefutable proof of immortality.

There is no way to prove to the human mind that there is such a thing as life eternal, and moreover, not only life eternal after what is termed death, but life eternal here and now, indestructible and immortal. The materially minded witness the ravages of disease, and they see the funeral ceremony and the body laid to rest, but because they are able to judge only by appearances, that is, by the seeing of their eyes, they receive no sign of immortality.

Those of illumined vision today, however, are able to see, not only that the "Pilates" with all their temporal power have not the power to destroy life, but that no form of war or physical force has the power to do this. Only the spiritually illumined can see that, for only the spiritually illumined can see beyond physicality to the truth that the material form is not the person. The person is *I*, and the physical form is but an instrument, like the bark on the trunk of a tree which is not the tree itself. The tree itself is invisible. The tree itself is the life which flows as the tree; and the trunk, the branches, and the leaves constitute the form, or the vehicle, as which the tree becomes visible.

ASSUME CONSCIOUS DOMINION

Of his life, Jesus said, "I have power to lay it down, and I have power to take it again."[3] Every one of us has a choice. We can either let the carnal mind—the belief in two powers—have its way with us, letting universal belief do anything it wishes to do to us, even to burying us at threescore years and ten, or we can take up our own life and determine: "I have God-given dominion over my body and over everything that is in this earth, above it, and beneath it."

If the body deteriorates, it is because we have not accepted spiritual truth, but have permitted universal belief to operate in, or upon, the body. Universal belief would instill in us the belief that weather can do one thing to the body; food or the lack of it, another; age or the passing of time, something else; and infection and contagion, yet another thing. All those are but part and parcel of the carnal mind, the universal belief in two powers.

If we do not take possession of our own life, and if we do not assume the dominion that God gave us, we are just like a limp cloth in the breeze which blows about any way the breeze wishes to carry it. Then, if universal belief says that this is the wrong climate, the body immediately responds with, "I have rheumatism"; if universal belief says that we are eating the wrong food, there is a stomach upset; and if universal belief informs us that we have reached threescore years and ten, we begin paying off the undertaker!

[3] John 10:18.

In every instance, we are obeying universal belief instead of the truth as revealed in Scripture, for Scripture states that God gave man dominion over the weather, over the food, over everything that is in the earth, beneath the earth, and in the heavens above the earth. Even the stars that so many people bow down to in worship and fear, yielding power to them— even over these man was given dominion.

I IS THE DOOR TO LIFE MORE ABUNDANT

Verily, verily, I say unto you, I am the door of the sheep. I am the door: by me if any man enter in, he shall be saved, and shall go in and out, and find pasture.

JOHN 10:7,9

Jesus reminds us that it is only possible to enter the life more abundant through the door, and then explains that this door through which we must enter in order to experience the more abundant life is a door called *I: I* am—*I* can lay down this life or take it up again; *I* have God-given dominion. As we ponder that word "*I*" and meditate upon it, realizing not only that *I* is something outside of the body, but also governing the body, all of a sudden we realize the infinite nature of the *I*. This is how Moses was lifted up from being a shepherd to being the leader of an entire people—just by the discovery of the meaning of the word "*I*." This is how a simple man who began life as a carpenter and who served as a Hebrew rabbi became the light of the world—all through the word "*I*":

I am the way and the truth and the life. I am that I AM. I am the bread, the wine, and the water. I have meat the world knows not of. I am come that I might have life and that I might have it more abundantly.

Anyone who realizes the sanctity of the word "*I*" becomes a leader, nation-wide or world-wide, of those who are seeking to find that life more abundant. It requires a realization of the meaning of the word "*I*," but that does not imply by any manner of means that it is easy to attain. It was not easy for Moses or Isaiah, nor for Jesus who made plain how difficult it was when he said, "Strait is the gate, and narrow is the way, which leadeth unto life, and few there be that find it."[4]

Even though it is difficult, however, with this realization of the true nature of the *I* that I am, it is possible for any individual to rise above the material beliefs of his particular age—above the domination of the carnal mind—into the dominion of the *I* that he is. It is possible for any person to die to his old materialistic concepts of life and be reborn through the realization of the nature of the *I* that he is. Once we recognize *I*, we are recognizing the presence of God, and "where the Spirit of the Lord is, there is liberty."[5] Wherever there is a recognition of man's oneness with his Source, there is the Spirit of the Lord.

THE OMNIPRESENCE AND INFINITY OF *I*

When we meditate on the word "*I*," having discovered that *I* is not in the body, we soon find that *I* occupies this whole room. Later on we discover that *I* is outside this room looking in, *I* is way up on the roof looking down, and sometime later we shall see that *I* am at the center of the universe, simultaneously looking forward, backward, to the left, and to the right, beholding this entire universe all at one time, including the past, the present, and the future, for I and the Father are one, and where God is, I am; where I am, God is.

"I am come that they might have life, and that they might have it more abundantly."[6] Where *I AM* is recognized, God is. In the recognition of *I* is the recognition of infinity, and as we ponder that word "*I*," we shall find that our life is becoming more abundant, our relationships with others more loving, peaceful, and generous, and our supply either increasing or else stretching further than it ever did before, coming to us with less effort, less exertion, less strain, and going out from us without any tenacious clutching of it to us.

[4] Matthew 7:14.   [5] II Corinthians 3:17.   [6] John 10:10.

We create our own pain by trying to hold on to form, by trying to hold on to things which we have outgrown, by trying to cling to conditions which, because they gave us joy yesterday, we believe will give us joy tomorrow, forgetting that we have been taught not to lay up manna for tomorrow, not to lay up treasure "where moth and rust doth corrupt."[7] We do not live on yesterday's manna; we do not live on yesterday's possessions: we live on, and by, the grace of God, but that can become apparent to an individual only when he has come into the realization of the nature of that *I*.

Many people lose the way because they think *I* lived only at one time and that two thousand years ago. They think *I* lived as the man Jesus and as nobody else, not realizing that *I* lives as you and *I* lives as me, and that *I* is the true identity of every individual. There is only one *I*, and we shall someday discover that that *I* is your being and my being and that It is ours in order that we might have life and that we might have it more abundantly. It is our permanent identity unto immortality, and if this temple of our body were destroyed, in three days, by our recognition of the *I* that I am, it would be raised up again. That is the whole meaning of the Resurrection.

SURRENDER YOUR BODY TO THE *I* OF YOUR BEING

"He is not here [entombed in this body]: for he is risen."[8] And we are not here in our flesh, because the moment we come into a truth-teaching, we have risen in some measure above the illusion that we are in a physical body, and we are beginning to perceive that our body is something within our own consciousness. That is what gives us dominion over it. It is within us and it is subject to the *I* of our being.

"I *am the way, the truth, and the life.*"[9] I *am the law and* I *am the resurrection. If you destroy this temple, in three days* I *will raise it up again.*

[7] Matthew 6:19.   [8] Matthew 28:6.   [9] John 14:6.

And so it is that by virtue of the *I*, which is Consciousness, we have dominion over this body. When it is sick, we can raise it up, and if it claims to die, we can lift it out of the tomb. "He is not here: for he is risen." The experience of Jesus should not be interpreted as the isolated experience of one man, because if it were, it would be of no value. Of what value would it be for mankind if one person were great enough to raise his body from the tomb, unless it was done as an example to show us the immortality of life and body and to show us that we have the power to be raised out of the tomb? By what power? By the power of *I*—by the power of Consciousness.

We have been given God-given dominion over everything there is, not by conscious thought, but by letting the body rest back in the *I* and then letting the *I* take over and govern it without any conscious thought on our part. We never have to tell the body what to do: we do not have to tell our heart to beat; we do not have to tell our digestive or our eliminative organs how to function; we do not have to tell any part of our body anything. We release the body into the *I* which is Consciousness, or God, and then let It function the body, for It is the infinite intelligence of the universe, and therefore It created this body and has the power to maintain and sustain it—*if* we release the body into It.

If, on the other hand, we attempt to assume control of our body by means of the human mind, we first have to determine how many times a minute we want the heart to beat, and then we have to be sure that it obeys, whereas the real teaching is to "take no thought for your life, what ye shall eat; neither for the body, what ye shall put on."[10] Our heavenly Father knows how many heartbeats we need, and it is His good pleasure to give them to us in full measure—He will not hold out one, nor will He give us one too many.

If we sit patiently and let *I*, Consciousness, take over, soon It will whisper, "Peace, be still,"[11] or, "*I* in the midst of thee am

[10] Luke 12:22.   [11] Mark 4:39.

mighty," or, "I am the only life, and I am infinite." Somewhere deep down within us, something will come into expression to assure and reassure us that we have surrendered ourselves to the Infinite Invisible, and in one way or another, It will let us know that It has taken over.

RELEASE YOUR BODY BACK INTO CONSCIOUSNESS

When a seed is planted in the ground, we do not tell the seed that it should come up as a rosebush and produce beautiful blossoms. We just surrender that seed to its own environment and wait patiently until a rose comes forth out of a rose seed. We are not surprised at all. That is what we expected and what we knew would happen because we were not attempting to govern or manipulate what was to take place in the ground. We plant the seed, obeying whatever we know to be the laws of planting, but then we let the law, the mind or intelligence, of this earth take over. We release that seed into whatever its native element or law may be, and we *let* whatever that law is govern it until it comes out as flowers or fruit or whatever its innate nature may be.

So it is with us. We take our body right out of the human mind with its belief in good and evil, and we place it where it belongs, in the Consciousness that formed it. How could it be in better care than that? We did not instruct the body to form a heart, liver, lungs, legs, eyes, ears, and hair. The *I* that I am has provided everything necessary, and when we place the body in its native element of Consciousness, from the depths of that Consciousness, comes the assurance, "I am on the field. Take no thought for your life, or for your body, because *I*, your heavenly Father, knoweth what your body needs, and it is My good pleasure to govern it."

Every day, we have to release our body back into Consciousness so that we are sure that our body is not being operated upon by human belief, because if it is, we are going to watch the body get sick, grow old, and die. And why should we be a witness to age and decay when, by turning our attention in the right direction, we can be a witness to the glory of God appearing as individual being?

"The earth is the Lord's, and the fulness thereof."[12] So I rest back in Consciousness and let Consciousness feed, support, maintain, and sustain me. I look not to *"man, whose breath is in his nostrils,"*[13] but I lean back in Consciousness. Thou, Consciousness, art my bread, my wine, and my water. Thou art my inspiration; Thou art the staff of life; Thou art the resurrection of my being and of my body; Thou restoreth the lost years of the locusts.

We take our body, life, and wealth right out of the human mind and place them where they belong in their native element:

God is my consciousness. I rest in God and I am fed by God, my Consciousness. The activity of my being, of my body, of my business, of my work, and of my home, I no longer place at the mercy of humanhood, but all these I return to the Father's house, and I rest in Thee.

Without taking thought, I learn to wait for the still small Voice, and It says, "Knowest thou not, I am closer to you than breathing, nearer than hands and feet? Knowest thou not that I am the rock on which you can rest?"

And then I feel something reminding me, "Whither shall I flee from thy presence?"[14] *Indeed, whither? I am always here in Thy Spirit, resting in Thee, relaxing in Thee. Thy grace is my sufficiency in all things—in bodily and in monetary affairs, in home and in family relationships. Thou, Thou art the activity of my being. I am rooted and grounded in Thee. I am the branch, Christ is the tree, and God is the ground in which I am rooted. From that infinite Ground, up through the roots,*

---

[12] Psalm 24:1.   [13] Isaiah 2:22.   [14] Psalms 139:7.

up through the branches and blossoms comes right fruitage.
It is Thy good pleasure that I bear fruit richly, and this I
do as long as I am rooted and grounded in Thee.

God is my supply; God is my health, my strength, and my
activity; God is the continuity and eternality of my being. God
is the rock on which I stand, my fortress and my high tower;
God is my abiding place where I live and move and have my
being—in Spirit, in Life, Substance, and Soul.

His wisdom is infinite, and all that the Father hath is mine.
By His grace, I have infinite wisdom. God has breathed the
breath of life into me, and therefore, my breath is really His
breath; my life is His life, infinitely harmonious, whole, and
complete.

ACROSS THE DESK

When understood, The Infinite Way will change the nature
of your prayers. Men have always prayed either to many gods
or to the one unknown God for better material conditions
and a greater abundance of things: the world has prayed
for bigger crops, for more rain and then again for less rain,
for safety, and for peace on earth. Men have prayed for homes
and companions and abundance until the world would have
been deluged with these—if the God to whom they prayed
were the kind of God who could answer such prayers.

Despite the billions of men and women who pray in public
places of worship and the other billions who pray alone, and
in secret, the sins, diseases, wars, famines, and storms continue,
and it would seem even increase. What explanation is there
other than that there is no such God answering such prayers?

The Infinite Way reveals that praying to God for anything
at all except for the one great gift of an understanding of
God is a waste of time. Throughout the ages, there have been
some who have attained God's grace and realized peace on
earth and an abundance of those things necessary to daily com-

fort; but it is always the attaining of a transcendental state of consciousness that is the secret of healing and harmony, and that spiritually enlightened consciousness is the substance, form, and activity of our immediate and continued good.

This message reveals how sincere seekers can attain some measure of this spiritual consciousness, and thereby bring joy, peace, health, and abundance to themselves and to all who can forsake the scramble for *things* in order to attain the awareness of the invisible *Substance* of things and conditions.

The error of the ages is the belief and the expectation that the ordinary material or mental consciousness can add to itself the blessings of God, whereas the truth is that only the children of God—those who have the Spirit, or consciousness, of God are heirs of God.

Before God's healing presence can be experienced, consciousness must be prepared—transformed, renewed, reborn of the Spirit—so that it may be a transparency for that Light, and God's grace may thereby find entry to "this world" and overcome it.

The Art of Spiritual Healing[15] sets forth the specific healing principles of The Infinite Way through which this mystical healing consciousness can be developed. The present volume, *Our Spiritual Resources,* is devoted to the actual revelation and unfolding of this transcendental consciousness through the understanding of Scripture and meditation. The Infinite Way "Wisdoms"[16] will be more clearly understood by using *Our Spiritual Resources* and *Living the Infinite Way*[17] will reveal deeper meanings, and even the tiny pamphlet *The Fourth Dimension*[18] will disclose its depth.

[15] Joel S. Goldsmith (New York: Harper & Brothers, 1959).

[16] Joel S. Goldsmith (San Gabriel, Calif: Willing Publishing Co., 1956), p. 156-192.

[17] Joel S. Goldsmith (New York: Harper & Brothers, 1961).

[18] Joel S. Goldsmith (Honolulu, Hawaii: Joel S. Goldsmith, 1956).

The world cannot know peace and oneness until we of the metaphysical movements attain unity in our relationship with one another. All those who stand for spiritual healing are *one* in spirit and in truth regardless of the differences in specific principles and the many different approaches to the subject of healing. The day of oneness is surely dawning.

CHAPTER V

SPIRITUAL ATTAINMENT
THROUGH PRAYER

Spiritual healing can be accomplished in several ways: It may come about through those who possess a healing consciousness, are fully aware of this gift which has been bestowed upon them through the grace of God, and use it to bless mankind; it may be experienced by some person who has no knowledge whatsoever of spiritual things, but who may have unknowingly brought himself within the healing orbit of God's grace; or it may be that a conscious knowing of the correct letter of truth, that is, the principles of truth, eventually leads to the development of that spiritual consciousness necessary for healing.

Since most healing is brought about through treatment, that is, through first knowing the correct letter of truth, every metaphysical student, regardless of which approach he chooses or elects to follow, should be able to give an intelligent treatment. This, however, has nothing to do with making affirmations and denials or uttering metaphysical clichés because such procedure is far removed from the giving of an intelligent and loving treatment.

65

All metaphysical teachings have as their goal the bringing of spiritual living into the experience of their students, and giving them some understanding of the nature of treatment, so that, through the practice of treatment, spiritual consciousness may be developed. The spiritual consciousness which is so essential to the healing work cannot be achieved through blind faith, however, nor merely by making metaphysical statements, even if, and though, the statements are true. Behind every statement of truth uttered and behind every treatment given, there must be understanding.

THE PRINCIPLE OF ONE POWER

No one can give a spiritual healing treatment intelligently unless, first, he anchors himself in the realization that since God is all power, there is no power that is required to do anything *to* anything, *for* anything, or *for* anybody, *for* any reason. We do not even need God-power, inasmuch as there is but one power, and that power is God, the Creator, Maintainer, and Sustainer of the universe. It is our responsibility to know this truth so that we do not go to God in an attempt to influence God to do something to us or for us, or to our patient or for our patient. We turn to God only for the assurance that God alone is. When we learn to do this, we will not fear infection, contagion, or anything that mortal man or mortal mind can do to us.

Human experience is a constant warfare between the power of good and the power of evil, the power of sin and the power of purity, the power of health and the power of disease; and were we to judge solely from the events confronting us in the world, evil is much more powerful than good because it usually seems to be victorious over good and seems to abound so much more than does good.

The end of our subjection to two powers began in the nineteenth century when the first of the metaphysical movements revealed that the thousands of years of warfare between good and evil had been unnecessary because there are not two powers: there has always been only one power, and that power is God-power, spiritual power. Evil was not, and never has been, a power, but only a belief entertained in human consciousness which acted as power so long as the belief remained in consciousness.

A new term, mortal mind, was coined to describe this belief in two powers which Paul had called the carnal mind. This carnal, or mortal, mind was proved to be no power at all. Instead it was demonstrated to be a nothingness, a belief entertained in human thought. All the evil—whether appearing as sin, disease, death, lack, limitation, storms, wars, or man's inhumanity to man—was to be understood as *effects* of the carnal, or mortal mind, which was not a mind, but a hypnotic influence.

This revelation resulted in remarkable healing work, behind which was a great principle: there is only one power, and that power is God. Every other so-called power, whatever its name or nature, is the carnal mind, or mortal mind, "an arm of flesh," nothingness. This understanding enabled practitioners to heal cases of cancer, consumption, and polio; it enabled them to stop infection or contagion before it could spread— not because infection and contagion were powers over which they could try to exercise control, but because these are not power, and such power as they seem to have exists only because they have been accepted as power in universal human thought.

Unfortunately, as this teaching became crystallized and more and more people began to accept it, mortal mind, which had been revealed to be a nothingness, began to be feared as a power, so that today in most metaphysical practice, there are once again two powers warring against one another—the divine Mind on one side, and mortal mind on the other side—instead of the great principle that God alone is power.

Let no one believe that a metaphysical treatment, no matter by whom given, is of any value whatsoever if it does not include an understanding and a conviction that there is only one power, and that this one power is not a power to be used over another power. Let no one think for a moment that he is of any help to his patients or students, if he is still expecting God to do something for them, or if he hopes and believes that his treatment is going to get God to do something for them. God's work is done. God is the same yesterday and today and forever, and let no one try to influence God on his, or anyone else's, behalf.

Into every treatment, we must put all the metaphysical understanding of truth that we have, and the most important point of all is to go into our meditation with an absolute and unshakable conviction of the one power and of the nothingness of that which appears as sin, disease, death, lack, and limitation. Unless this all-important step is taken, the treatment is incomplete and is not really fruitful.

SHAKE OFF INERTIA AND GAIN DOMINION

It is the degree of realization that determines the efficacy of the treatment. We do not all have one hundred per cent success in our treatment or healing work. In fact, I know of no one who has as yet attained one hundred per cent, although this is possible if the full Christ-consciousness of one power can be attained and, if instead of refuting, denying, or struggling against error, the full truth of Jesus' teaching, "resist not evil,"[1] can be realized. Would the Master have admonished us to resist not evil, if evil has any power to exert over us?

No treatment will ever result in any better healing than the nature and quality of the treatment given, because there is no mysterious God sitting around waiting to do our work for us. God is doing God's work, creating, maintaining, and sustaining this universe in perfect harmony. Discord and inharmony are known only to us—they are unknown to God—and they

[1] Matthew 5:39.

are known to us only in the degree that we live and move and have our being outside the divine awareness, permitting ourselves to be influenced by what we see, hear, taste, touch, and smell.

A human being is much like a weather vane, swinging this way and that, according to the accepted beliefs of the moment. He is not in control of his own life or body, but is swayed by the universal beliefs current in human consciousness.

Such was not the original status of man for, in the first chapter of Genesis, he was given dominion—dominion over everything on this earth and beneath it and above it: we were given dominion, but have we not given over that dominion to the weather, to economic conditions, and to governments, so that today we have formed the habit of looking everywhere outside ourselves for the complete dominion which really should be coming forth from within ourselves?

It is possible to regain that dominion, but it can only be done through conscious effort—conscious, determined, persistent, consistent effort—and in no other way. Inertia is really in control of the human mind, and before we can gain the desired dominion, we must overcome that inertia and really work for that dominion.

The first step in shaking off the inertia which seems to hold us in its grasp is to learn the basic principles of truth and put them into practice. Unfortunately, too many students believe that merely learning what these principles are is sufficient, but if there is to be an expanding spiritual consciousness, they must be practiced by living them and by using them in treatment. While it is true that, if we give enough treatments over enough years, eventually our treatments will have far less of words and thoughts in them, that will only be because those words and thoughts have become thoroughly ingrained in our consciousness, and not because we can ever feel so satisfied with the degree of our spiritual attainment that we can afford to skip or omit them.

THREE PRINCIPLES BASIC TO SPIRITUAL HEALING

The nature and purpose of treatment is to bring us to that state of consciousness in which God is realized. Therefore, when we go into treatment, which is a preliminary to prayer, we must make use of the correct letter of truth contained in the principles of The Infinite Way.

The first of these principles has to do with the nature of God. The spiritual healer must have a sufficient understanding of the nature of God to be able to relinquish, or let loose of, his old concept of prayer and be satisfied to go to God without asking Him for anything or expecting anything of Him beyond what He is already doing. There must no longer be any attempt to influence God in anyone's behalf—not even his own.

The spiritual healer will not use truth to overcome error, nor will he expect God to heal disease, reform sin, or exchange lack for abundance, because any spiritual healer worth his salt knows full well that God is already performing Its functions: God is eternally bringing forth all the things that not only are needed today, but which will be needed in the farthest future of which we can conceive.

The second important principle constituting the letter of truth is the instant recognition of the impersonal source of all the evil that has ever tempted man. Evil is never anything other than a temptation, a suggestion or an appearance. Regardless of the name or nature of the particular discord that confronts us, our patients, or our family, whether it is some form of sin, disease, or lack, we must remember that it has its basis in an impersonal source which we may call devil, Satan, or the carnal mind. It makes no difference what name is used as long as we understand it to be impersonal and from an impersonal source.

When that is thoroughly understood, coupled with an abiding conviction of its truth, we are ready for the third basic principle of spiritual healing as taught in the message of The Infinite Way: since God did not create the carnal mind, that impersonal source of evil, the carnal mind has no cause; it has no life, no law, no substance, no activity, no avenue and no channel of expression. In other words, the evil which appears as person, place, thing, circumstance, or condition, and which to our dulled perception apparently has power, is a nothingness, the "arm of flesh" which Hezekiah cautioned his people not to battle, because the "arm of flesh" has no God-power, no God-ordination, no God-substance, and no God-activity.

An understanding of these principles enables us to withdraw from the battle so that we do not fight evil, thereby obeying Jesus' great teaching, "resist not evil." The moment that we can come into the presence of any form of evil with a relaxed mind, a mind that does not attempt to jump up and begin battling and denying it straight off, we are ready to see it dissolve into its nothingness. But if we take out our mental sword and begin to deny and argue against the evil, or if we attempt to overcome some power, we are lost.

The correct way to approach any and every form of evil is with the realization, "The cause is causeless, an appearance, an impersonal source of no power." This is the healing principle of The Infinite Way. It is not a truth that overcomes error, nor is it a God that will reform, heal, support, or supply us. The God of The Infinite Way is already maintaining and sustaining us in our spiritual perfection, and our task is to awaken from the belief in two powers and begin to honor God by respecting the first Commandment: "Thou shalt have no other gods before me"[2]—thou shalt acknowledge no other powers besides *Me*. How can anyone fear an evil power if there is only one power and that one power is God?

It is only in the honoring of that First Commandment that students can begin to perceive the healing principles of The Infinite Way. And how do we learn to obey this great Com-

[2] Exodus 20:3.

mandment? How do we learn to "have no other gods before me"? How do we learn to honor God above all else? It is at this point that every student must make use of his mind as an avenue of awareness and as an instrument of God.

Mind imbued with the truth that there is only one power is a law of regeneration, resurrection, and renewal. Therefore, your mind imbued with truth can be a law of harmony unto my body, unto my business, art, or profession, and unto my welfare. In the same way, my mind imbued with truth becomes a law of harmony unto your body, your business, being, happiness, freedom, and welfare, and in proportion as my mind is imbued with truth, do you receive healing and Grace. Similarly, in proportion as your mind is imbued with the correct letter of truth, and then ultimately with the consciousness of truth, does your family benefit, and eventually your patients and students.

MIND IS THE SUBSTANCE AND ACTIVITY OF THE BODY

Most physical problems are in some way related to the organs and functions of the body, and whenever such a problem is presented, the treatment must include the truth that mind is the substance of the bodily organs and functions. There is not a cell of the body—not a cell of the bones, the flesh, or the blood—that is not a center of intelligence, which it could not be unless its very nature were mind. The secret is not mind over matter, but *mind formed as matter*.

The organs and functions of the body are not something separate and apart from the mind. Therefore, it is of little value merely to try to improve the body, unless first of all we understand the activity of the mind. If anyone for a moment believes that the organs and functions of his body are not responding to the acitivity of his mind, he has not yet awakened to the basic truth of metaphysical practice which is that mind is the substance of the body.

An intelligent, efficacious treatment must include the truth that mind activates the organs and functions of the body, that mind flexes and relaxes the muscles of the body, and that the body of itself can do nothing or be nothing.

The mind prepares the way for every experience that comes to us, even though, as truth-students, we are prone to ignore the Master's statement that as ye sow so shall ye reap, and to feel in our egotism that this really was not meant to apply to us. But let us not fool ourselves. The body carries out the directions of the mind, and what the body does must first be thought, or accepted, in mind.

This is not to be interpreted as meaning that if lack is being experienced, it is because of a thought of lack, or that if an automobile accident occurs, there has been a conscious thought of an automobile accident. It is not quite as simple as that because what is in operation in the world is an *impersonal universal mesmerism* which has been foisted upon us and accepted in the mind from infancy. These *universal* beliefs, *which constitute this mesmerism*, act upon the body through the mind and must be recognized as no power because of the allness of God and our oneness with that All.

PERSISTENCE AND PRACTICE LEAD TO DEMONSTRATION

Let us not believe for a moment that there is some kind of an unknown power operating for your good or mine. There is no such power: the power is a conscious realization of truth. Certainly, those who have already mastered the art of meditation and are at that point in their meditation where God announces Itself, so that they know that they have the God-presence with them, do not need to know as much of the letter of truth because they have already attained God Itself. But most people find that that experience comes to them very seldom. Seldom is it that they really feel that the place whereon they stand is holy ground, or that they really have that inner conviction that "where I am, God is," or that they hear that still small voice.

If we hope to attain greater God-consciousness, it means that we have to devote more hours of the day, more days of the week, and more weeks of the month to a conscious practice of truth. We have to take these principles and work with them individually and specifically until we feel that we have voiced or thought them all, so that now we stop for a moment and say, " 'Speak, Lord; for thy servant heareth.[3]' I am waiting for Thy voice." Then we sit for a minute or two in a receptive consciousness and sometimes we actually feel that the Spirit of God does touch us.

There are other times when we have no feeling that God is on the field and when there is no such conviction. It is as if the treatment were a failure as far as we are concerned. But that is not true. The treatment is never a failure as long as we have done our part, and if there is no outer change, we are willing to do it again two hours from now.

Too many students think that if they give themselves or others one treatment in a day, the rest of the day is up to God. No such set program can be followed rigidly. I have seen some very serious claims met in something less than a treatment, but on the other hand, I have seen some very simple things that took days, weeks, months, and sometimes even years of work before a healing took place. Sometimes the patient or even the practitioner himself blocks the healing by holding on to self-will in some way, or by holding on to some other thing which he is not yet ready or willing to loose.

This is a spiritual universe, a universe which God made and which, when He looked at it, He found good. The discords, the inharmonies, and the injustices are not in the world: they are in our misperception of the world—in what we are seeing and hearing with our human sense of sight and hearing. Are we listening with the physical ears or with the inner ears? Are we seeing with the human eyes or with the inner eyes? With our five physical senses, we will always behold degrees

[3] I Samuel 3:9.

of good and degrees of evil. It is only when we penetrate into the Withinness, unleash our divine faculties, that we see this universe as it is, and then, regardless of the sinner or the dying person at whom we may be looking, the voice within says, "This is my beloved Son, in whom I am well pleased."[4] But we shall never see the "beloved son" if we insist on seeing with the physical eyes and hearing with the physical ears because we can never know God's grace or God's kingdom with the five physical senses.

Let us understand very clearly that knowing the letter of truth in treatment is not really the spiritual healing agency. The function or purpose of knowing the truth is to set our mind at rest so that the divine Consciousness can manifest Itself in, and through, our mind and thought. For example, we can never find inner peace while we are trying to get a great power like God to do something to error or while we are expecting God to give us supply, companionship, or a home. We shall find inward peace only when we are willing and able to surrender human desire, turn within, and realize, "God is my need and God is the fulfillment of my need. My only desire is to know God whom to know aright is life eternal."

One of the deepest truths of the Bible is that to know God aright is life eternal—to know Him aright is infinite abundance, to know Him aright is to know love, to know Him aright is to know divine harmony. But to seek for harmony separate and apart from Him, to seek for health separate from Him, or to seek for supply separate and apart from Him is futile and useless.

One thing only do I desire: to know Thee aright, whom to know aright is life eternal. May the thoughts of my mind and the meditations of my heart be acceptable in Thy sight.

And they will be acceptable if we go to God as an emptiness and in the realization that there is no God-power to do some-

[4] Matthew 3:17.

thing to somebody. God-power is to be realized as the sum and substance of individual being.

These truths, taken into consciousness, constitute seeds of truth, and if we nurture them—feed and water them by remembering them—they will spring forth into spiritual demonstration. Day after day, we must take the important points of the correct letter of truth into conscious treatment.

Never should we leave home in the morning without establishing within ourselves the realization that what we see, hear, taste, touch, or smell cannot sway us since we are receptive and responsive only to the divine Influence within our own being:

God's presence is with me: It is beside me; It goes before me to make the crooked places straight; and It comes up behind me as a rear guard.

God permeates not only my being, but all being. God fills all space, and my conscious realization of this is a law of protection unto everybody who comes within range of my consciousness—even the drunken driver just ahead of me or on the other side of the road. The mind of God, acting in and as and through individual consciousness, is the mind of every driver on the road.

God is here where I am, for I in the midst of me is God.

Until you have made this kind of treatment a matter of conscious realization, you have no security out on the street, or anywhere else because you will just be going about as an ordinary human being—as a statistic. Take possession of yourself: take possession of your mind, your heart, and your Soul—but do it consciously. Do not be vacillating about it. Be positive.

We have dominion, but we have dominion only in proportion as we assume that dominion through truth, always remembering that of our own selves we are nothing. I am speaking of the dominion that we have through truth realized in consciousness, of the infinite abundance that is ours by God's grace—by grace of the truth that God is our being, and that we are, or can be, transparencies through which the activity of God is made manifest to this world.

As "the heavens declare the glory of God; and the firmament sheweth his handywork,"[5] so must you and I bear witness to God's glory—not to your glory or mine. Never bear witness to your knowledge or your powers. Give God the credit for being the infinite and all-Spirit.

Of all the spiritually dedicated men and women I have met in the course of my travels, I have yet to hear one of them admit or imply that he felt spiritual. So do not be misled into believing that you are ever going to feel spiritual. You are just going to feel that you are you, but if you let yourself be the transparency for the Spirit within, that spirituality will flow through you, and as you, and by its fruits in the experience of those who touch your life, you will know that it is there. You, yourself, will not feel it, any more than an honest person feels honest. You can never *feel* honest, but you can *be* honest. If you could feel it, you would be feeling honesty in comparison with dishonesty, so there would still be remnants of dishonesty lurking in you by which you could make that comparison.

No one in all this world ever receives a spiritual blessing or benefit for his own sake alone. Any spiritual blessing that is ever given to us by the grace of God is for the benefit that it will be to this universe. Of those who have much, much will be expected and demanded. Nobody is ever given the grace of God and then given permission to go up into the mountain and hide somewhere with it. The more of realization we have, the more activity is given to us through which to use our understanding and development for the benefit of this world. One thing alone counts, both in spiritual living and spiritual healing, and that is the truth we know and how steadfast we are in its application and practice.

[5] Psalm 19:1.

Human nature does not accept easily or readily such a program as is outlined in this chapter, nor does it relish the prospect of such work, but it has no hesitancy whatsoever in admitting that it wants to enjoy the fruitage of the labor when the work is faithfully done. Out of the study and practice of such lessons, comes the attained illumined consciousness which in turn appears as the harmonies of life.

Our illumined consciousness, the fourth-dimensional consciousness, is the very substance of our health, success, and wholeness. Our realized consciousness is the health of our countenance, the fortress and high tower of safety, security, and peace. Keep in mind that our illumined consciousness does not give, send, or provide us with any of these things, but rather that this consciousness is itself the divine activity, substance, and law of our being.

The Master does not teach, "I will give you food, water, wine, eternal life, or resurrection," but he teaches, "I am these." He reminds us to labor not for the forms that perish —for the *forms* of good—but for the attainment of God-realization so that we may abide in the assurance that where I am, all good is, because I am there. Where I am, all that I am appears as the forms necessary to my experience. Without taking thought, and only because I am, all that I am appears in good time and in abundance.

My realization that where God is, I am, and that all that the Father has is mine is the transcendental consciousness which lives my life, going before me, appearing as many mansions, and where necessary as "by day in a pillar of a cloud . . . and by night in a pillar of fire."[6] Once the consciousness of God's grace is established within us, our life is lived "not by might, nor by power"[7] but by this Consciousness Itself.

[6] Exodus 13:21.   [7] Zechariah 4:6.

CHAPTER VI

DOMINION OVER MIND, BODY, AND PURSE

A thorough understanding and practice of the subject of treatment is one way of rising into the true atmosphere of prayer and God-consciousness. Treatment means consciously knowing the truth and applying the principles of truth through the instrument of the mind, and the first step is to establish yourself in your true identity as *I*, that *I* which has dominion over mind and body. Until you do that, you cannot give or receive a correct treatment.

You were given both a mind and a body. The mind is not you, nor is the body: *I* am you, the *I* which is your true identity. Your mind and your body are something that you possess. The mind is the instrument which you use for thinking or reasoning purposes or for any purpose of awareness, and it is through your mind that you are able to judge and make decisions.

The body is also an instrument, a physical instrument, which takes its orders from you through the mind. You say to your hand, "Up," and the mind communicates that to the hand; the hand obeys the mind which in its turn obeys you, indicating that you must have control over both mind and body.

The mind and the body were given to you, and dominion over both of them was also given to you. If, however, you do not exercise that God-given dominion, you soon find yourself in all kinds of trouble.

When you sit down in meditation, the mind usually is far from still, not because it has a wish or will of its own, but because you have not assumed dominion, and the mind is conditioned to becoming a prey to any and every universal belief floating about in the atmosphere.

It is much like the horses that I have ridden. They do not acknowledge my control a bit. Instead, they take me where they want to go, but that is only because I do not know how to assume dominion over a horse—and so he has his fun with me. So it is true that the mind also has its fun with us, but only because we have not learned how to exercise dominion over it.

In some ways, the body behaves better than the mind and is far less obstreperous. At least, the hands will not steal if we do not direct them to do so, and the hands will co-operate, share, and give, if we so direct them; but the body can be just as unruly as the mind: it tries to determine for us when we are well and when we are sick, as if we had no dominion in the area of physical well-being. Yet, rightly understood, we have as much control over our health as we have over our morals or as we have over the thinking mind, and the only reason we do not seem to have it is because we have not assumed dominion.

This dominion can be compared to the loving control that a wise and emotionally mature parent exercises over a child. It is a discipline of love and gentleness, exercised in peace and with patience.

ASSUMING DOMINION OVER THE MIND

One way to learn to exercise control over the mind so that you can meditate more successfully is by gently addressing the mind in some such fashion as this:

*I say unto you: "Peace, be still—peace, be still. Fear not,
God in the midst of you is mighty. Fear not, not even all
the armies of the aliens, for God in the midst of you is mighty.*

*"God's peace give I unto you, my mind—God's grace give
I unto you. In quietness and in confidence shall you meditate,
and in stillness and in joy shall you receive God's grace. Peace
be unto you. My peace give I unto you.*

*"You need not battle. You need take no thought for what my
body shall eat, nor what it shall drink, nor wherewithal it shall
be clothed. God's grace clothes me and God's grace feeds me.*

*"Be still and receive God's communion. Be still and hear the
still small Voice. You need not battle."*

*Nothing shall enter my mind that defileth or maketh a lie.
No weapon that is formed against me shall prosper. I need
not fear what mortal mind can do to me for it has only the "arm
of flesh," whereas I have the Lord God almighty.*

*"Where the Spirit of the Lord is, there is liberty"[1]—there
is peace, harmony, quietness, calmness, and assurance. "Where
the Spirit of the Lord is," there is God's presence, and in His
presence is fullness of joy, fullness of life, and an abundance
of good. Here where I am, God is.*

In this meditation, you take possession of your mind and
acknowledge that peace comes, not by virtue of any qualities
of your own, but because of the presence and grace of God.
You have realized your identity as separate from the mind and
body, as having jurisdiction over both mind and body, and
through that practice, you have assumed dominion.

Living as most people do in the hustle and bustle of modern
life, they do not realize that there is something beyond the
mind and body called I, and because of their ignorance and
their inability to recognize this something, the mind and body
seem to constitute all there is to them. In other words, there is
no recognition of a Being superior to the mind, exercising
dominion. In our work, it becomes necessary to realize that

[1] II Corinthians 3:17.

our real name and the real name of all the Bills or Marys of this world is *I*, born of God, created in His image and likeness, God maintained and sustained. By the grace of God, each one of us has a mind and a body. These are our instruments given to us for specific purposes on earth.

MEETING FINANCIAL PROBLEMS

The value of all this you will soon see when you are faced with a problem, whether your own or one concerning somebody who has turned to you for help. Let us assume for the moment that a problem of supply has been brought to your attention.

To begin with, never under any circumstances is the patient taken into your treatment—neither his name nor his image is permitted to enter your thought. As a matter of fact, if he does not reveal his name, you do not ask for it. You are not interested in the name or human identity of any person, because your work has nothing to do with personalities, although the people who bear those names will receive the fruitage of the work.

How is that possible? How do they receive the benefit of the work instead of someone else? Because they have brought themselves to your consciousness and made themselves a part of it by asking for your help. It is "thy faith [that] hath made thee whole."[2] So, if a person asks you to give him help, even if you do not know his name, what he looks like, or anything about him which might identify him as a particular individual, he has made the necessary contact and will receive the help because the person himself—his name or his body—does not enter into the treatment in any way.

When you are asked for help on the subject of supply, there is only one thing that you can do, and that is to turn away from the person and the problem, and immediately begin to know

[2] Mark 5:34.

the truth consciously. You must not take either the patient or the claim into your meditation; you cannot take lack or limitation, nor can you work on the subject of either lack or abundance.

Then what truth should you know? Your consciousness has just been given a temptation in the form of a miserable appearance, and so you must know the truth, but not the truth about the problem because there is no truth about a problem. The problem must immediately be recognized as temptation, the carnal mind, having no substance, law, or cause. The only truth there is, is the truth about God, the truth about the spiritual universe and individual being, and that truth is this:

"The earth is the Lord's, and the fulness thereof."[3] *God does not belong to anybody, and neither can the earth belong to anybody. This earth is God's footstool, and all that is therein. God constitutes this universe, God's presence fills it, and God is the only life, the only law unto it, and God is the only supply. God constitutes the fulfillment of all being.*

Then, as you begin to dwell consciously on truth, you begin to remember many passages which bear out the fact that God alone is, such as, for example, "I am the meat; I am the wine; I am the water." Where is there an absence of I? Where is there an absence of God? I fills all space. I is here and I is there, and I is everywhere.

Do you see that your treatment consists of statements of truth, but never statements on the level of lack or limitation? They are always on the level of spiritual truth, because you are consciously knowing the truth about what constitutes supply which is the truth about God, the fullness of God, the omnipresence of God, and the omnipotence of God.

The remembrance may come, "Man shall not live by bread alone, but by every word that proceedeth out of the mouth of

[3] Psalm 24:1.

God."[4] Where is there an absence of God's word? Only with those who do not abide in the Word and let the Word abide in them, only with those who do not dwell "in the secret place of the most High."[5] With such, there is an absence of supply because they are cutting themselves off from the only supply there is, the word of God which is the bread, the meat, the wine, and the water.

THE PRINCIPLE OF SUPPLY

If the world is to be awakened to the true nature of supply, it will first have to learn the principles from those who have discovered them and are practicing and demonstrating them. If only those who are reading this chapter were really demonstrating supply spiritually, it is not difficult to imagine how many of their neighbors, friends, and relatives would clamor for a knowledge of this truth. But abundant supply cannot be demonstrated unless we ourselves know the principle of supply and, knowing it, let that principle be operative in our treatments every single day of the week, month after month, until it is demonstrated.

The principle of supply can be stated in a few words, but it takes years to put it into practice, and even then this is possible only if we are willing to break through inertia sufficiently to give not only ourselves, but our friends, relatives, and enemies a good treatment every single day until this treatment becomes realized consciousness. After that, it is only necessary to remind ourselves occasionally of this truth in order to stay in the Spirit.

And what is this principle of supply? It is that God is the only supply there is. Neither money nor investments are supply. Money comes and goes; investments come and go; real estate, too, comes and goes, fluctuating in value. There is only one supply which is permanent, and that supply is God. That supply is not only infinite and eternal, but it is also omnipresent and

[4] Matthew 4:4.   [5] Psalm 91:1.

unchanging. God realized is infinite, omnipresent supply.

Truth-students who try to demonstrate supply from any other basis are doing nothing more than is the human being who is a good go-getter. Through their efforts, they may demonstrate a little temporary money or property, but that is not supply. Supply is never supply until it is ours forever and forever in infinite abundance—a sufficiency with twelve baskets left over to share.

God, alone, is supply and if that premise is accepted, then its corollary must also be accepted: to have supply one must have God. Too many people glibly repeat, "God is everywhere, equally present." That is true in the abstract. That is a very good absolute statement of truth, but it may result in a very bad demonstration, because God is not omnipresent until God is realized. If the truth of God's omnipresence were all that is necessary to provide abundant supply, then all the poverty-stricken people of China and India would be overflowing with supply because God is omnipresent in those countries as well as in this one. But that is not enough. God becomes a demonstrable experience only in proportion as God is realized. God is present without measure throughout this entire world, but it takes an individual imbued with this truth to bring forth the healing.

If you keep your treatment on the level of God, on the truth of being, away from your patient and his problem, you will eventually reach the place where you come to an end of thoughts and words, and then you can settle back for the second half of your treatment. Here, too, The Infinite Way is unique in that it does not consider a treatment of any value in and of itself, but only as a stepping stone to the second part of the treatment in which you are through with words and thoughts, and relax, waiting on God, "It's Your turn, now, God. Speak to me; I am listening." And then there is that period of silence for which you have prepared yourself and are now ready after you have devoted adequate time to knowing the truth consciously. In that moment of expectant waiting comes that inner peace, that "click," that something or other that enables you to know that God is on the field, not God mentally declared, but God spiritually realized. Then you can go about your business, and your work is complete.

MEETING PHYSICAL PROBLEMS

The next problem that may come to you may be a physical one: the organs or the functions of the body are not doing their job, or the blood system, the muscles, or bones are undergoing some form of deterioration. Let me remind you once again that before you sit down to your treatment, you should have eliminated your patient's identity—you no longer have him in thought because your treatment has nothing to do with a patient: your treatment has to do with knowing the truth, and there is no truth about your patient, or he would not be a patient.

In knowing the truth, you will forget what he has told you about his body. It makes no difference to you whether it is a condition of the heart, liver, or lungs, because you are not a physician and you do not even know that the difficulty lies in the heart, liver, or lungs. Many people who develop a little pain in the area of the heart immediately diagnose it as heart disease and then perpetuate it by holding it in their thought. Actually, the patient may not have anything remotely resembling heart disease, so it would be nonsensical for you to sit down and work on heart disease every time someone told you that he thought he had a weak heart.

Your job is to forget the claim as fast as it is unloaded on you. Forget the identity of the patient. For many years, I have recognized how important this is, and that is one of the reasons why there are no books and no records in my office of those who come or call for help. The only time a name appears on my office pad is when I have an appointment and have to make a notation of the day and the hour. But there are no other names or lists of treatments, no list of names to whom bills are to be sent, no record of names at all, and certainly no record of claims.

You have been asked for help on a physical problem, and as you sit down to give your treatment, you should immediately forget who has asked for the help and why he has asked for it, although the fact that it is a physical problem may remain in your consciousness. Your first thought probably is, "The body, in and of itself, cannot be sick. There is no sickness in the whole kingdom of God." That wipes out that possibility at once. Now you can forget even the word "sick" because now you know that there is not a trace of sickness in the entire kingdom of God. If there were, there would be no immortality, there would be no eternality, because sickness eventually leads to death, and so there cannot be sickness in the kingdom of God.

The only place there can be any sickness is in the mind of man, and the mind of man is not a creator. It is the mind of God that creates, not man. Therefore, man cannot create a disease: the best he can do is to create the belief that he has one.

There is no sickness in the entire kingdom of God because the kingdom of God is a kingdom of immortality, eternality, life, and love. Under Moses, there was the law, but under Jesus Christ there is Grace. The kingdom of God is a kingdom of Grace, not of law; and therefore, in the kingdom of heaven there cannot be laws of matter or laws of mind; there cannot be laws of weather, laws of climate, or laws of food; there cannot be any laws of limitation because the whole kingdom of God is a state of Grace. We are no longer under the law, we are under Grace—we have come out from under the law and have become separate.

Do you see where you are in consciousness now? Not once has your mind gone to the person or to his claim. Instead, you have tabernacled with God—you have kept your conversation in heaven. Now you can sit back peacefully, "It's Your turn now, Father. I'm listening." You will find that with a few moments of that quiet and peace, something will come to you from within—some feeling, some words, some message, some light—and you will know that God is on the field, and a smile will come to your face.

GOD, THE ONLY POWER

Another person comes to you and asks for help, and this time something he has written or told you brings to your mind the thought that there is an apparently negative power, an evil power, a sinful power, or a diseased power operating in his experience. Immediately, you turn from him and his claim to that word "power." This is an easy one to deal with because you would not be this far along on the path if you did not believe in God as the one and only power.

In fact, those of us who are on the spiritual path have gone beyond a belief in God to a conviction—if not to the very experience itself—that God is. With such a conviction, the treatment will be a very short one, because if God is, there is no power but God. That can be the only meaning of God—infinite Power, Omnipotence, which rules out the possibility of there being a material or a mental power.

It is true that in the human picture, you are always being presented with the power of the human mind and the power of matter. Only when you come to the kingdom of God and have risen above the pairs of opposites can you say with genuine conviction, "Since there is a God, there is no material or mental power, unless these are instruments for God, and then they are of the nature of God—good."

Surely you know that there is no evil or destructive power if there is a God. Does God exist? What is the nature of God? If God is not infinity, if God is not immortality, if God is not omnipotence, and if God is not omniscience, God is not God. But if God is these things, there is no such thing as a destructive, harmful, or injurious negative power.

When you have established within yourself that God is and

that there is no other power, you have given your treatment. Now you are ready again for that period of listening in which the seal is placed on that particular treatment.

A TRANSFORMATION OF CONSCIOUSNESS IS REQUISITE

Every practitioner has had the experience of working with apparently obstinate cases. Such cases are most frequent with patients who believe that they can just go on being ordinary human beings and still add to their humanness God's grace. Too many people really believe that all they have to do is to come to some truth-teaching and find the right person who can say the right words or do the right thing, and then the blessings of God will descend upon them. That is far from true.

The human being has to yield himself to God. There has to be a transformation of consciousness in the patient himself, a yielding of the mortal sense in order to make room for spiritual awareness. It does not always follow that this transformation comes with the first or second healing, nor even with the third or fourth. Often students have several remarkable demonstrations, or healings, and then later on they find that the truth does not seem to "work" any more. What has happened is that they have been benefiting by the practitioner's state of consciousness and, after a period of time, they may come to the point where even the work of the most dedicated practitioner is ineffective.

There may be different reasons for this, but undoubtedly one reason is because some students do not yield themselves to truth, and there is no surrender of self. It is possible that the practitioner through his own dedicated life can free an individual from many of his trials and tribulations, lacks and limitations, sins and diseases, but if the patient continues in his old human way for too long a period of time, he may find, not only that the truth does not "work," but that sometimes things so much worse come upon him that he might even wish he could return to the original error.

Paul taught that human beings are not under the law of

God and cannot be, and that human beings cannot receive God's grace. It is possible to become the son of God only as we permit the Spirit of God to dwell in us: "But ye are not in the flesh, but in the Spirit, if so be that the Spirit of God dwell in you. . . . For as many as are led by the Spirit of God, they are the sons of God."[6] Jesus gave it to us in yet another way: "Love your enemies, bless them that curse you, do good to them that hate you, and pray for them which despitefully use you, and persecute you; That ye may be the children of your Father which is in heaven"[7]—pray for your enemies, not for your friends or relatives, but for your enemies.

The principle behind that is this: If you have been lifted to a place in consciousness where you can seriously and honestly pray that your enemies be forgiven, that they be released from punishment and from their sins, that the Spirit of God enter their Soul and mind and being, and that they be given release from these mortal claims, you are no longer a mortal. When you approach the level of consciousness where you make the transition to Christhood and are able to say with the Master, and mean it, "Forgive seventy times seven. . . . Resist not evil," you have yielded your humanhood. You have yielded *your* will, *your* opinion, *your* convictions, and you have accepted the grace of God, and the Spirit of God does dwell in you.

The Spirit of God does not dwell in a person filled with envy, jealousy, malice, hate, or revenge. If you feel that you are now yielding up whatever human emotions of a negative nature you may have indulged, you yourself can know that you are now in an atmosphere that is not only receptive and responsive to spiritual healing, but you are now approaching the state of consciousness which can do healing work.

There are many people, totally unprepared, who go into the healing work in the metaphysical world, and who engage in it merely because they believe they are qualified by right of having a title or a degree or an authorization. That does not

[6] Romans 8:9, 14.   [7] Matthew 5:44, 45.

make a healer. No number of titles or degrees has anything to do with a successful healer. A healer is one who has yielded up so much of his humanhood that he is able to forgive seventy times seven, to pray for his enemy, to resist not evil, and to put up the sword of antagonism, hate, envy, jealousy, and malice. When a person has yielded up all these traits which the majority of human beings love to hug to themselves, the Christ has taken over his consciousness, filling it full of the "forgive-thine-enemies" state of consciousness, and then he is prepared not only to be healed spiritually, but to heal.

There is no doubt but that in every one of the metaphysical and spiritual movements there are practitioners who have attained enough of this measure of Christhood, or Christ-consciousness, to be able to heal. It makes no difference through what approach they come. What counts, and what is important, is the degree of spiritual consciousness they have attained because that is what determines their healing ability.

This realized spiritual consciousness is a recognition of *I*. There must always be an *I* with complete dominion over mind and body, so that when the student sits down to give an intelligent treatment, that is, consciously to know the truth, the mind or the body will not keep him from his duty or his obligation, which in the end becomes his privilege and pleasure. "Thou wilt keep him in perfect peace, whose mind is stayed on thee."[8]

And how do you come to know these truths that you must consciously declare? You must live in the Word, and let the World live in you, so that you will have at your mental fingertips every passage of truth necessary when you sit down to give a conscientious, intelligent treatment.

ACROSS THE DESK

Let us stop for a moment and look at the human scene, not because it is so pretty to look at, but because we cannot over-

[8] Isaiah 26:3.

come it without some measure of understanding of its operation.

A human being can never be certain that any given day will not contain for him an accident, an illness, a temptation, or a loss. These things are happening every day to countless numbers of people, and no one knows when one or more of them will come nigh his own dwelling place.

When a person learns the cause of evil and knows why these experiences continue to occur in human life, he learns how to meet the problems of each day and thereby attain freedom, harmony, joy, and peace—and what is even more important, he is equipped to serve his family, his neighbor, community, nation, and world.

In The Infinite Way, the student learns to face each day with the *conscious* realization of the impersonal nature of evil and of its impotence: he *consciously* knows that I *am* is God. Therefore, I am one with God, and the place whereon I stand is heaven. He realizes that where God is, I am; and where I am, God is, for we are inseparably and indivisibly one—"Son, thou art ever with me, and all that I have is thine."[9] This truth is a universal truth.

Evil, regardless of its name or nature or its specific form, is impersonal, and therefore has no person in whom, on whom, or through whom to operate, and not being ordained of God, it has no spiritual law to uphold or enforce it. It is the "arm of flesh"—temporal power, nothingness. To abide in this truth is to be clad in the spiritual Robe where none of these things shall come nigh thy dwelling place.

The Infinite Way student is taught that whatever he experiences must come through his own consciousness, and that, therefore, to fill consciousness with an understanding of the nature of God and a knowledge of the impersonal and impotent nature of the cause of evil is to ensure a life of spiritual harmony and service to others. The student who omits this daily, conscious abiding in truth subjects himself to the universal belief

[9] Luke 15:31.

in two powers, but the belief in two powers cannot operate in a consciousness that has realized God as Omnipotence and Omnipresence. Were it not for this acceptance of the belief in two powers, there would be no human existence, and we would all be living in a heaven on earth. Our immunity from material conditions and our freedom from mental laws are attained in proportion to our daily and hourly conscious remembrance of these revelations.

God gave us dominion over every circumstance, but we must exercise that dominion by an active, continuous consciousness of the truth of our oneness with God, and by the conscious and specific knowing of the impersonal and impotent nature of the source of error. To lay the ax at the root of material existence is to understand it as a product of mental suggestion, having no law or authority.

To live the life of Grace is to realize consciously that *I* is God, and *I* in the midst of me is the meat the world knows not of—the hidden mystery of life eternal, harmonious, and spiritual.

CHAPTER VII

LIVING BY MEDITATION

There comes a time in the lives of all those who reach out to God when the experience of God-realization takes place. Although it is literally true that God fills all space and that where we are, God is, this has little significance in the life of the average human being, because the activity of God does not come into anyone's experience until God has been *consciously realized*. It is an actual experience, and at the moment of its taking place, we know that it has happened.

Because of the pressure of human life, however, this God-experience does not remain a permanent dispensation. It is possible to have the realization of God, thereby experiencing God's grace, and yet, a day or two later, find ourselves leading much the same kind of a human life as before, with just as much of chance, change, or accident in it. It becomes necessary, therefore, to renew the experience of God-realization, not only every day, but very nearly every hour of every day, because there is a tremendous amount of world pressure in the atmosphere which unconsciously we pick up and to which we respond unknowingly from morning to night and from night to morning.

Even those who are far along on the spiritual path will acknowledge that there are times when, for no known reason, fear grips them, or when doubt and uncertainty may overwhelm them; and this is nothing more nor less than the activity of world thought which intrudes into the consciousness of every individual, although this is true to a far lesser degree of those who remain, insofar as possible, in God-consciousness, that is, those who learn to "pray without ceasing."[1]

There are two approaches to life—one in which life is lived by the law and the other in which it is lived by Grace. Life lived on the human, materialistic level is difficult at best and oftentimes not only difficult, but to many actually unpleasant. It is a life lived by the sword, not merely the sword of war, but also the sword used in business, the sword of competition —stiff competition, clever competition—and in social life, the sword of seeking status at almost any cost. And yet, Christ Jesus taught that those who live by the sword will die by the sword: "Resist not evil. . . . Ye have heard that it hath been said, An eye for an eye, and a tooth for a tooth: But I say unto you, That ye resist not evil."[2] To the human sense of life, these are strange words, well-nigh impossible ones for some to follow, because all of human existence is made up of resisting or fighting something—always that "eye for an eye."

How can a person go from the state of consciousness in which life is a continuous battle, lived by competition and by the sometimes devious modes and means of human experience, to that life by Grace in which there is no need to take thought for what we shall eat or what we shall drink, or wherewithal we shall be clothed? Is such a way of life possible? Does anyone live without taking thought, without struggle, or without strife? Does anyone live without the use of force or might, purely by the Spirit of God?

THE ALCHEMY OF ILLUMINATION

If we study carefully the lives of the ancient mystics and even some of the more modern ones, we cannot help but

[1] Thessalonians 5:17.   [2] Matthew 5:38, 39.

observe that they had just as much trouble and anxiety, just as many earthly woes as most of us experience until, on a specific day and on a specific occasion, they received illumination or, in other words, the direct experience of God.

It was through such an experience that Gautama became the Buddha, the Enlightened One, and after that experience he was able to heal and teach the spiritual wisdom with which he had been endowed. People came from all over India to seek him out, to learn of him, to be healed, and to be given instruction in spiritual living. What a great light he must have been that the fame of his illumination could spread so far and wide that it brought to him people from all parts of that vast subcontinent, seeking to partake of his light—and all this within a short space of time, and without benefit of newspapers, telephones, television, or radio.

The experience of Jesus Christ five hundred years later was undoubtedly even more phenomenal. Here was a man, born of lowly parentage according to the human sense of values, a man who was a carpenter and a Hebrew rabbi authorized to teach and preach in the synagogues, but who later became the Christ. What could have brought about this radical change from an itinerant Hebrew rabbi, walking up and down the Holy Land, preaching by the sea, to becoming the recognized Saviour of the Christian world?

Certainly, a tremendous transition must have taken place in his consciousness to have lifted him out of the temple, because otherwise he would have remained as his fellow rabbis remain, unknown. But an experience took place within him—of the how, when, or where of it, there is no definite knowledge— a transition took place which made of Jesus, the Christ, made him the light of the world, a light that has not grown dim in nearly two thousand years, even though few there are who have really seen that light.

To all appearances, Moses was an ordinary individual although in a higher strata of society than other Hebrews of his day;

but he was nonetheless a man of common clay and a man of irascible temper. Yet this man led the entire Hebrew people out of slavery, not only into physical freedom, but into a higher sense of religion than these people had ever known. Was it a man of the Court, an ordinary Hebrew, a man of clay like everyone else who did this? No, Moses did not play any such significant role until he had had an experience on a mountain top, which perhaps may not even have been an actual mountain, but unquestionably was a mountain top of spiritual realization.

From the moment of his illumination, however, he was no longer a shepherd or a man of clay: now he became the man who was able to break the power of the Pharaohs and to lift a whole people out of their environment, lead them across one of the wildest wildernesses imaginable, provide for all their needs—see that they were fed, and that they had water, safety, security, and protection through all the dangers—and take them almost to the Promised Land.

Elijah was persecuted and finally forced to seek sanctuary in the wilderness, but through his illumined consciousness he, too, found safety, security, and supply ever at hand wherever he traveled.

Do you not see that these men—and there are hundreds more of whom this same story might be told—through their moments of illumination were lifted above being the man of earth to become that man who has his being in Christ, and from then on they stood head and shoulders above the throng, teaching, healing, and lifting others out of the ordinary human experience into a higher dimension of consciousness.

Every one of these spiritual lights gave his light to thousands of others and made it possible for the apostles, disciples, and those who were to come after them to follow in some degree in their footsteps and live their lives also by Grace. But then what happened? Often within a couple of generations after these great mystics had left the scene, their followers began enjoying the effects of their teachers' spiritual experiences instead of living in the consciousness which produced the fruitage of the Spirit, and soon they were lost once again in their materiality.

AN OVERTURNING IS NECESSARY TO AWAKEN MAN OUT OF HIS INERTIA

The human mind, dulled by inertia, has no desire to think; it does not want to discipline itself or to be disciplined. That is why there are so few executives and so many clerks; that is why there is only one great doctor among the hundreds of mediocre ones, one great statesman among thousands of politicians. The human mind does not wish to be disciplined; it does not wish to labor or to hold itself to principles: it prefers rather to follow a policy of drift.

In order to rise out of the indolence characteristic of the human mind, there must be an overturning, and an overturning, and an overturning, until He comes whose right it is. Let us not look upon this "overturning" as a collective experience, but rather as an individual one.

To you and to me, there will be a continuous overturning in our consciousness until there is a dawning of that spiritual realization which is necessary. This means that we may take one step forward and fall three steps back, that we may go forward and almost reach our goal, and then fall back into sin, disease, or lack, or perhaps experience so much material affluence that it drives us even further back. Surprising as this may seem, lack is not our worst enemy, nor is disease. Sometimes health and prosperity can be far more detrimental to our spiritual progress than lack and disease, because it is in health and prosperity that we seem so able to do without God. Things have a way of going on beautifully by themselves until—and then there is another overturning.

The overturning continues until one day, because of some sin in our experience, some disease or lack, and in a few cases because health and prosperity prove to be unsatisfying, we come to that point of wondering, "Is there not some place beyond this? Is there not something beyond this?" Oh, yes, we hastily agree that we believe in God and that we know there is a God, although we are not quite honest enough to add, "But only because I'm afraid not to believe for fear of what might happen to me." But that really is the situation in many cases, until the inner drive, and sometimes the drive from outside, comes, and the search begins.

It really makes little difference what path one chooses when the search begins. A person can begin, if he is fortunate, with the highest mystical teachings, or he can begin with the most paganistic of religious teachings and sometimes even with atheistic teachings. The label is not important. What is important is that he has the intention and desire to find God—to realize God. With that for a goal, regardless of how many sideroads or blind alleys there may be, ultimately he attains the goal.

It is possible to talk about God and to think about God, but that does not bring God into our experience, although it may be a prelude to the experience. The praying, the thinking, and the speaking—even the reading about God—will not bring the experience of God. God comes into our experience in a moment of silence. That moment may last only a hundredth of a second, if there is such a measurement of time, or it can be the blink of an eyelash, but no one can know either "the day [or] the hour wherein the Son of man cometh."[3] In that one second, when the human mind is still, the experience of God comes.

That is where contemplative meditation plays its most important role, because the practice of meditation leads us to that point where the mind can become still. It is not really possible to still the human mind or to stop its action, although there are countless exercises and practices aimed at accomplishing this, practices which may result at times even in some form of mental aberration.

[3] Matthew 25:13.

To live in the beautiful passages of the Bible and the inspired literature that comes out of the heart, mind, and soul of God-realized men and women, however, quiets the mind and finally brings it to a stop, even if only for a second or a tenth of a second—and in that second there may come that blinding flash. It may be as blinding a flash as the one which turned Saul of Tarsus into St. Paul, or it may be an insignificant little second of light that makes us say, "I think that was it; I hope it was, but it was gone so quickly I was scarcely aware of it."

Remaining in the Word—reading spiritual literature, pondering its meaning, and meditating over it—leads us to that inward stillness and quiet, to those moments of peace which bring us to the period of meditation when the experience of God can take place. From then on, it is a simple matter to bring it back again, time after time, until eventually living in that fourth-dimensional life becomes an almost continuous experience.

Usually, however, because of the indolence and inertia of the human mind, the student will not do the one thing necessary to keep himself on the path until this moment of transition can take place. Nothing can happen to a person except what happens within his consciousness. Therefore, for the spiritual student, there must at all times be an activity of truth in consciousness. Remember that statement, because it is important and vital to spiritual progress: *There must at all times be an activity of truth in consciousness.*

If truth is not actively maintained in consciousness, life becomes one of futility, a waiting for something to happen. The hoped-for and long-awaited spiritual awakening, which many people desire, but toward the attainment of which they make no effort, does not happen except perhaps once in a hundred years, or possibly to one out of a million persons, and even then, as we know from the history of many to whom it has happened, it is of no value, because it came unexpectedly without understanding and without any idea or knowledge of how to recapture it.

KEEP TRUTH ACTIVE IN CONSCIOUSNESS

If we maintain truth consciously active in our consciousness, however, we shall ultimately arrive at a place where the activity of truth will come into our consciousness of its own accord, and then thereafter we shall be fed by it instead of our feeding our mind with it. We shall find ourselves awakening in the morning and *consciously* remembering:

"This is the day which the Lord hath made."[4] *This is God's day, and God's function is to be with me to guide, lead, direct, support, maintain, and feed me. "Thou wilt keep him in perfect peace, whose mind is stayed on thee."*[5] *Right now my mind is stayed on God, and I acknowledge God in all my ways.*

I acknowledge God as the divine Presence of this day; I acknowledge God as that which gives us our sunshine, our rain, our food, our inventions, art, literature, and music. I acknowledge God as the Source of all that is.

At breakfast again comes the recognition:

The Lord hath indeed set a table before me, and I acknowledge God as the Source of the food that I eat.

When leaving our home for business, or whatever the activity may be, instead of just walking out of the door, truth should again become active in consciousness, and we should realize:

He goes before me to make the crooked places straight; today He performs that which is given me to do; He perfects that which concerns me. Yes, even if I walk through the deepest of valleys, He will be with me. I shall fear no evil—no infection, contagion, or accident. I shall fear no evil, because His presence is with me.

Business problems, household problems, family problems—these, like the poor, are always a part of human experience, but

[4] Psalm 118:24.   [5] Isaiah 26:3.

always there is a spiritual truth with which to meet them. For example, there are people in our social and business life or in our professional life with whom we are not congenial, and it becomes our function to remember that God is as much the life of these individuals as God is of our life, and God is as much the mind and the Soul and the love of these individuals as God is the life and the mind and the Soul of us. We are one in Christ—not two.

There is no occasion any hour of the day for which Scripture has not provided a spiritual truth that can be our meat, wine, bread, and water, our rock, our fortress, and our foundation. We can always find refuge from any phase of discord in the fortress which is the word of God, and we can always rest secure on a foundation that is built on the word of God.

The degree in which truth is kept active in consciousness determines not only the degree of our ultimate spiritual illumination, but the time of it. It could be tomorrow, next week, next month, or next year; but that moment we determine by whether or not truth is kept active in our consciousness for an hour on Sunday, an hour every day, two or three minutes out of every hour in the day, or ultimately with almost every breath we breathe. It is possible to "pray without ceasing" if we know the inspired passages of Scripture and those of mystical or metaphysical writings, if we are willing to remember to apply them, and, above all, if we are able to overcome the inertia of the human mind.

SOW THE SEEDS OF TRUTH IN SEASONS OF PLENTY

It requires a one-pointedness and a dedication to remember not to jump out of bed in the morning without having first devoted a few minutes to a conscious realization of these truths. It takes long practice before one can sit down to breakfast without forgetting to realize the Source of the food on the table before him. Today, that table may be set in the midst of abundance and plenty, yet one never knows when it may be in the wilderness; but wherever and however it is set, the same principle that can provide a table in the midst of a present abundance can also provide it in the wilderness, if, but only if, we have learned to abide in the Word.

Is it possible to experience too much of discord or inharmony if we are abiding in the realization that God is closer to us than breathing, that the place whereon we stand is holy ground, or that if we make our bed in hell, even there God is? But think now of the discipline that is necessary to abide in those statements when we do not need them and when all is going forward smoothly. Unfortunately, far too often we do not take the trouble to remember those reassurances when we have no need of them. Who needs to think about God in the midst of him when he is walking down the avenue on a bright sunny day and when the worst thing that can happen is a little rain, or "liquid sunshine"? But if we would remember on those walks that, if we mount up to heaven where we are right now, God is with us, and that if by chance we should be called upon to walk through the depths of hell, He would be there too, then when these untoward experiences arise, consciousness is alert and ready to respond with, "Fear not. I am in the midst of you, and I am the power."

All these spiritual truths—scriptural and metaphysical—maintained in our consciousness, iterated and reiterated, eventually become a law to us, taking root in consciousness. I like to refer to these metaphysical and spiritual statements as seeds of truth which we take into our consciousness in our seasons of plenty. It is then that they take root and grow and eventually become fruit in the season when we need fruit, that is, when we need the Word. Moreover, the very act of maintaining our consciousness filled with truth tends to quiet any inner fear or doubt which may arise.

It is not that you or I fear anything or anybody, but nonetheless there are times when we entertain fear for some reason or other, although actually this fear has nothing to do with you or with me. It is a universal thing out in the atmosphere, and the whole world is filled with fear, fear as to whether inflation is going to destroy investments, fear of the unemployment still in our midst, fear of disease, epidemic, and disaster. Fear is now, as it has ever been, one of the most devastating emotional experiences of the human world, and unless a spiritual defense has been built within us, those fears will translate themselves to us as discordant experiences.

The earth is full of sin, disease, death, lack, and limitation. The promise is, however, that these will not come nigh our dwelling place, *but only if our dwelling place is in God.* Sin, disease, death, lack, and limitation cannot reach God, and those who are hid with Christ in God, those who live and move and have their being in truth, are the ones who are immune, and if not totally immune, at least immune from eighty or ninety per cent of the world's problems.

After a period of consistently maintaining these truths in consciousness, we find ourselves settling into a state of real peace—no fear is entering, there is no concern about tomorrow, and we are absent from the body and present with the Lord. Into that moment of quiet, stillness, and peace, there comes a realization of God's presence which, even though it may last but for a fraction of a second, we know has been the experience of God.

These periods of communion with God prolong themselves. Sometimes it seems that we have meditated for only five minutes, but when we look at the clock we find that a whole hour has gone by. Then we understand why, when Jesus was in the wilderness, he was anhungered. He probably had been in meditation for several days before he had any thought of food.

GOD MUST BE EXPERIENCED

As long as God remains just something to think about or talk about, it is similar to mere talk about any subject. For example, Victoria Falls in Africa, with its tremendous scope, the thundering of the water as it drops, and the unimaginable grandeur of the surrounding scenery, is an interesting subject for conversation, but when one has finished talking about it, one has not yet experienced Victoria Falls, and it still remains nothing but an idea or picture in the mind, and a very inadequate picture when compared with the reality.

So it is with God. As long as we are talking about God, thinking about God, or reading about God, it is all very beautiful, but God is still a million miles away—just a picture in thought, an idea, but not an experience. It is when we have finished with the talking, the thinking, and the reading, and are in that moment of inner stillness that the experience comes, and then we understand what it means not to live by the law, but by Grace.

When Grace touches us, we do not take thought for our life, and yet nevertheless wonderful things are taking place in our lives, things which come to us as a gift of God, and we realize, "This is something I had nothing to do with, and so this must be a pure gift of God."

Living in this state of meditation and returning to it a dozen times a day, so as to re-establish ourselves in that inner peace, God's grace flows to us, and in turn flows out from us to bless others, and always without effort, without strife, and without struggle.

CHAPTER VIII

BRINGING GOD INTO
DAILY EXPERIENCE

 B ringing God into individual experience is possible only through an activity of consciousness. If we make a conscious contact with our Source, we make contact with the spiritual Source of all those who can bless us and all those whom we can bless: "I in them, and thou in me, that they may be made perfect in one."[1] That relationship of oneness is not really effective, however, until the moment of contact, because until that moment we are separate human beings, each with his own interests and purposes, each with his own needs, and in that separateness we may not be fulfilling one another's needs at all.

There is no circumstance in life so small or insignificant but that it can be made an important one through that conscious contact. If it were nothing more than the routine of merely going out to market, it would not only save time, but what is more important, making that conscious contact even in inconsequential matters would establish in us the habit of making and continuing the contact so that when some more vital decision or problem arose, there would be no possibility of forgetting

[1] John 17:23.

the principle, because our reaction to it would have become more or less automatic.

It may not be too important to us whether our marketing costs eight dollars or eight dollars and sixty cents, and it may not be too important whether we buy this cut of meat or that one, or whether we purchase these vegetables or those. The important thing is that we are forming one more link in our chain, because we shall be learning never to make a move without a consciousness of that oneness. There must be the actual experience of being consciously one with God in order to find ourselves consciously one with all spiritual being and idea. Declaring it with the mind is not going to make it so, but if we keep that principle in our mind, sit with it, reflect upon it, and ponder it until we feel that inner response within, then we actually begin to demonstrate our oneness with all spiritual being.

It is that experience of God-contact which lives our life. Up to that time, truth is merely a statement in the mind, and a statement in the mind is a far cry from demonstration. It is when the statement in the mind becomes a feeling in the heart that we know that we have hold of the hand of God and the hand of God has hold of us.

ESTABLISHING GOD-CONTACT

Before engaging in any of the activities of our day, we should make it a point to establish that contact with God. For those who have not yet learned how to do this, in the beginning, it will take time. It may be necessary to read for a few minutes and then sit and meditate for a few more minutes, then read again and meditate, ponder some truth, and again meditate. It may take a whole hour before we really get the feeling, "It is done."

Those of us who are busy with the activities of daily life and meeting the pressing demands of this world may raise the question, "Where do I get that hour?" That is a matter for each one to determine for himself. Every person has to decide whether attaining this Christ-realization is worth getting out of bed an hour ahead of time or two hours ahead of time, or whether it is more important to have that extra sleep.

There is no one who can legitimately say that he does not have enough time because everybody has twenty-four hours in the day, and while each person may have demands made upon him for perhaps at least twelve of those hours, during the other twelve, he undoubtedly has the choice whether he will watch television or listen to the radio, go to a movie, sleep, or spend at least two of those hours trying to reach that feeling of oneness with God. Each one must determine to what extent he really wants this experience.

A God-contact is not merely a statement in the mind: it is an actual inner release from worldly fears or cares, and it is followed by further spiritual light and then gradually by a change in body, purse, or in other circumstances. When we have achieved this actual realization, we shall know that we are being divinely led, divinely protected, or divinely instructed, and that God is on the field in whatever the situation may be.

There is one point that will help to bring this realization of divine guidance and protection to us more quickly than any other, and that is this: the longer we persist in believing that God heals, enriches, or supplies, the longer we shall be left outside the realm of demonstration. We must come to a place where we realize that God is not a power: God is a presence. God is a power only in the sense that God is a creative principle, the power that maintains and sustains Its creation, but God is not a power in the sense of, "Oh, if I could just contact God, He would heal everybody, supply and protect everybody I know." God is not a power in that sense.

God is a presence, but because God is a presence, and infinite, there is no other presence. All sin, all disease, all death, and all lack disappear before God's presence. Therefore, we must be very careful when we are meditating that we do not believe that God's power is going to heal somebody, or that God's power is going to provide supply, or that God's power is going to result in somebody's being employed. It does not operate that way.

GOD APPEARS AS

God is "the health of my countenance."[2] If that is true, we do not try to get a God who is a great big power to remove disease: *we merely get God.* When we have the realization of God, that presence of God realized is the health of our countenance. It does not establish health; it does not make for health: it is health. God is health, and besides God there is no other health, so there is no use ever trying to attain health; but in attaining God, we shall find that God is the health of our countenance.

In spite of all the teaching to the contrary, God does not give supply, and God does not send supply, and God does not bring about supply: God Itself is the supply. When we have the feeling of God's presence, we have all the supply there is, and there is no other. The supply of God's presence is all we shall ever need or want, because when we have that we find that all things are included in it. There is no such thing as God *and* supply. God Itself is supply and when we have God, we have an infinity of supply.

Let us never believe that God is going to find a pleasant, comfortable, beautiful house for us to live in: God is our dwelling place. We should not want a house and we should not want a God to get us a house: all we should want is God Itself, and we shall find that when we have God, we have a dwelling place that to our friends and neighbors will appear to be a beautiful home, a practical, useful home, or a home rightly situated.

If we are trying to find a home separate and apart from God, or trying to find a house *through* God, we may be surprised how many centuries we shall have to wait for that demonstration; but when we give up the desire for the home or the house and have the desire only to know God aright, our home or house

[2] Psalm 42:11.

will appear automatically, because God is our dwelling place. There is only one place we should want to live and that is in God. We should live and move and have our being in God and stop thinking about places and houses and cities and locations and center our attention on one thing:

God is my dwelling place. My only need, then, is God—not a dwelling place, but God. When I have God, I not only have the dwelling place, but I have all that is necessary to establish that dwelling place, to furnish and maintain it.

In the same way, God does not provide us with safety or security, and praying to God for those things is a complete waste of time. God Itself is our high tower; God Itself is our fortress. Therefore, if we pray for the realization of God, for the realization of Omnipresence, we shall find that even though we walk up and down the street without any physical protection, our spiritual protection will guarantee that no evils of the world will come nigh our dwelling place. How can they, if our dwelling place is God? It is when our dwelling place is some place other than God that accidents can happen. But if we are consciously dwelling in the secret place of the most High, if we make God our abiding place, if we make God our high tower and fortress, if we make God our supply, if we make God our health, then we have no need of dwelling places, fortresses, health, or supply, because in attaining God-realization, all these things are included because *God is those things.*

God cannot send health; God cannot provide supply; God cannot ensure safety or security or protection; God cannot even bestow wisdom: *God is these.* Therefore, with all our getting let us get God, only God, and the realization of God's presence. Then we shall find that God interprets Itself to us in terms of practical living, so that if we were in the woods, as Elijah was, and there were no other way of being fed, we would find ravens bringing food to us, or we would wake up and find cakes being baked on the stones right in front of us, or, like Moses, alone in the wilderness, manna would fall from the sky. In other words, none of these people ever concerned himself with the demonstration of things.

When the Master multiplied loaves and fishes, he did not multiply loaves and fishes: he looked up to heaven. In other words he realized God's presence and God's grace, and then automatically the loaves and fishes were multiplied. We can not multiply loaves and fishes, and Jesus himself did not multiply them. He realized God as Omnipotence and Omnipresence, and that realization translated itself into what we understand as the practical things of daily life. Similarly, if we need employment, It leads us to our employment; if we need a home, It leads us to what appears as our home; if we need supply, It releases it in one way or another; if we need friendships or family or if we need somebody to do something for us, It performs all of that for us.

Do not try to seek supply separate and apart from seeking God, and above all do not try to *use* God as a means of providing you with home, companionship, or health, because you will be making a servant out of God, and God can never be that. You cannot use God, or Truth; but God, or Truth, can use you. God, or Truth, can manifest Itself in you and through you.

THE PRINCIPLE OF ONENESS IN SALESMANSHIP

If a salesman were to make his contact with God in the morning before leaving home, and left for work with the feeling of God's presence beside him, within him, and around him, he would automatically be spiritually at one with those who needed what he had to sell, and in the course of the day, he would be led to them. In proportion to the depth of his contact and to his continued ability to listen, he would be led to his customers without waste of time, and then it would not be necessary for him to make ten calls in order to make one sale.

In my own experience, on two different occasions, I had the opportunity of proving this principle. In the particular field of selling in which I was engaged, the salesmen were taught that normally there was one sale to an average of twenty calls and that if a salesman would conscientiously make twenty calls in a day, he would make one sale; if he made forty calls, his average would be two sales a day. This average was so well established that sales managers used it as their guide to determine the amount of time their sales people were working; but this norm was completely reversed when I proved that one call could result in twenty sales—not twenty calls in one sale. By making the contact with my spiritual center, I was not only one with God, but I was one with all spiritual being and idea, so that usually when I made my call and my sale, there were enough recommendations growing out of the one sale to result eventually in twenty.

Later, during the early days of the depression when I was in the practice of spiritual healing, a man who was selling a particular service and who found at that time that nobody was able to buy this service came to me for help. As a result of that help, he was able to apply the same principle and prove that whereas ordinarily five calls resulted in a sale, the process was reversed, and one call resulted in five sales. Moreover, because of his phenomenal success with this principle, within less than a year he was promoted to the position of sales manager in that organization.

Salesmen often seem to be subjected to particular stress and pressure because, first of all, not only is there the problem of selling the merchandise, but also of ensuring its delivery. Moreover, in selling merchandise, there is always a third factor to be considered, the all-important one of the buyer, and if the salesman is living merely as a human being, he is competing for the sale of his merchandise not only with every other salesman handling similar lines but also for the buyer's favor, and finally he is competing with other salesmen in his own company to obtain prompt and safe delivery.

All this can easily and quickly be changed provided there is a change of consciousness on the part of the salesman. When a salesman is able to lift himself above the human picture by realizing that there is only one power, one life, and one activity, and that limitation, cut-throat competition, and sharp business practices are but the carnal mind, he discovers that there is only one buyer, and that one is God appearing as a thousand buyers. Therefore, it is to God that he offers his merchandise because God is appearing as infinite individual being—as salesman and as buyer.

Furthermore, everything that exists is an activity of God and a creation of God, so whatever it is he may be selling—mechanical gadgets or clothing—it has all originated in consciousness. God is the originator, the creator, and the designer, and certainly God never created any item to stand idle on someone's shelf in a store or warehouse. The very realization that God is the creator of any particular piece of merchandise should be sufficient assurance that God has created an outlet for it—effective advertising, the proper display of the product, and the right buyer for it. The entire activity is going on in the consciousness of God, not in the consciousness of man.

The owner or manager of a store may believe that he is limited to the customers of his immediate neighborhood, but there are thousands of people operating out of some little neighborhood store or office who have proved that their customers may be scattered all over the world—Africa, Asia, and Australia; whereas possibly even in the very same neighborhood and at the very same time, there may be others who cannot draw enough from their own community to support them.

SPIRITUAL PRINCIPLES RELATED TO BUSINESS

The pressure of business activities can be dealt with through the application of the principles of spiritual healing to any particular business situation: God appearing as individual being, the impersonalization of any discordant, limited, or limiting condition, and the "nothingizing" of it by realizing that there is only one power—and then falling into the rhythm of God-living, instead of human living.

For example, a businessman who goes to his office is usually faced with many different kinds of problems in a day: there are decisions to be made and obligations to be met, and there are his associates and the public with whom he is dealing constantly making demands upon him.

Perhaps one of his first duties is to answer his mail which may be a time-consuming or even a disturbing responsibility. If, however, before leaving his home or even after arriving at his office, he takes a few minutes to commune with his inner being and finds his center of peace within, then when he opens his mail it is as if there were a Something within him reading it and supplying him the answers to whatever inquiry or problem may confront him.

When we understand that God is the activity of business, all sense of pressure is relieved because then we are permitting this invisible Something to operate and perform whatever is necessary. Jesus called It the Father within who does the work; and if God, the Father within, does the work, how can we feel any pressure in our business? If we feel burdened and under pressure, whether we are willing to admit it or not, we are attempting to take over God's responsibility. The government is on His shoulders, but if we are not acknowledging and relying on that, then we are assuming a responsibility which does not belong to us.

If we were to adopt the role of a beholder in our business and were to watch the activity of this Infinite Invisible unfold, we would soon find that It would unfold as whatever was necessary to Its fulfillment—as capital, if our business needed capital, as employees, as buyers, and finally as payment in the bank for the merchandise.

In other words, the activity would be a complete one because the nature of God is fulfillment. God does not create a telephone system and no one to use it; God does not create automobiles and no fuel with which to make them run. God does not create or become responsible for any activity in our consciousness without fulfilling it. God, the divine Consciousness, the Infinite Invisible, fulfills Itself as individual activity.

SERVICE SHOULD BE THE MOTIVE IN BUSINESS

Most business enterprises are undertaken because those organizing or sponsoring them anticipate deriving benefit—profit or satisfaction—from them. Such a narrow concept, however, is not the truth about business, and to entertain any such concept would be as erroneous as to believe that a physician thinks that his patients come to him in order to enrich him. Few doctors feel that way. The attitude of most doctors toward their patients is, "Thank You, Father, for the opportunity You are giving me to help these people." If the medical practitioner becomes rich through his practice, that is certainly legitimate, but only incidental to the service he is performing.

Why should not business concerns have this same attitude? For example, when a customer enters a department store, why is not the atmosphere charged with the thought, "Thank you for coming and giving us the opportunity to provide what you need. That we will make money through the transaction is incidental to the fact that we have the joy and opportunity of serving you. We are here for that purpose, and the income derived from the enterprise is only in proportion to our service to you."

Spiritually speaking, every business transaction is performed for the benefit of the public concerned, whether it is an article of clothing, a book, or a new heating plant. Whatever it is, the object in the business world should be to serve the needs of the customer and feel when he comes into the shop, "Thank you for giving me this opportunity of blessing you." The businessman who takes that attitude need never worry about failure or bankruptcy. If a man is in business, he should make it a matter of specific treatment on his part to realize every day: "I'm going to my place of business to serve the community, not to make money or to get rich. Therefore, I must have a clean window, a clean door, and a clean shop, and make it such a pleasant place to come to that all those who enter it will be blessed."

This may not sound or seem like a very practical approach to what most people consider the hard and insensitive world of modern competitive enterprise, but nevertheless many well-known and highly successful firms have been built on just such a principle of service.

Business is not cold; business is not cruel; business is not mercenary except in those cases where the heads of the business have not learned the spiritual principles of life. The man who has learned these principles should remind himself of them, keeping them uppermost in his consciousness, realizing that whoever enters the door of his business is entering the door of his consciousness, and that he must therefore meditate in order to have the presence of God there for his customers and associates to meet when they enter his consciousness. Every businessman should make it his business to meditate before he goes to his business, so that everybody who comes into his consciousness finds God waiting to greet him.

Once we realize that our conscious oneness with God constitutes our oneness with all spiritual being and idea, and as we learn to establish ourselves in that oneness, we shall literally prove that there is Something that lives our life for us, Something that goes before us to make the crooked places straight. Then we are not living our own life. Now there is Something within us that gives us a divine intuition, an adequate warning of when not to take a step or when to take the next step forward so that many of the troubles of life can be avoided and, if and when it seems impossible to avoid them, It will quickly take over for us.

As we practice the Presence and make contact with the Spirit within, we find ourselves moving in a spiritual rhythm that carries us forward. There is an awareness of a Presence, of Something flowing in and through us. Soon we realize that It carries the responsibility, It carries the weight—no matter how heavy the load. It does the work, and that relieves the pressure while we, in turn, become beholders, witnesses, standing a little apart and to one side watching our life unfold.

ACROSS THE DESK

Our work would not be wholly successful if, only individually, we attained the Spirit of God and did not at the same time attempt to lift all men up to that same level of consciousness. Because of the change of time in different parts of the world, it is well to remember that when you are in meditation other Infinite Way students somewhere are in meditation at the same time, thereby forming a united conscious awareness of God's presence. When even one attains the realization of the Presence, all others are simultaneously lifted above the level of their present state of consciousness to the higher consciousness attained by the one.

Here also you have revealed to you the secret of supply. Supply can only be spiritually demonstrated on a permanent basis by rising in consciousness to a level above that which produced the lack. As long as one's consciousness remains the same as the one which suffers lack, the lack will remain. It is for this reason that it is futile to try to demonstrate supply. Demonstrate a higher, deeper, richer consciousness of God, and supply will flow at the higher level of consciousness.

The higher consciousness is attained by the study and practice of specific spiritual principles and by abiding in the inspirational literature of The Infinite Way message. Your meditations will lift you to the apprehension of spiritual truth, and this inner attainment will appear outwardly as form.

Remember that you are never meditating alone. You are always in and of the consciousness of those Infinite Way students, teachers, and practitioners who are in meditation with you at the same time all around the world. When you attain a measure of God-realization, you carry those in meditation right up with you. When another attains the presence of God, you are lifted to his level of consciousness—and with signs following. This consciousness is God's grace flowing as your divine sonship.

CHAPTER IX

INDIVIDUAL DISCOVERY OF TRUTH

Listory is filled with accounts of men who have conquered the whole known world of their day and yet who themselves have known only unhappiness, dissatisfaction, and a gnawing lack of peace; just as today, there are men and women who have attained everything that the world has to offer in the way of wealth and fame, and even with all their success they still know no peace. It is not that there is any evil in gaining the health or wealth of this world, nor yet in achieving the fame this world has to give; but, in and of themselves, not all of these together comprise a fulfilled life unless they are accompanied by something else. Of themselves, they cannot satisfy.

Because of this sense of lack, primitive men made gods for themselves. There was an inner compulsion to find an anchor in something greater than themselves, and so they created gods to reign over every activity of life—the crops, weather, love, vitality, home. In the case of the early Hebrews, when the one God was preached to them, It was not preached in such a manner as to be within the comprehension of the ignorant or unenlightened thought of that day. Therefore, in the absence of true spiritual leadership and because of their need for a God, they made for themselves a golden calf, for men have always found it necessary to have something to worship, and so, when they did not find the true God, they fashioned substitutes in order to avail themselves of something which would provide hope and temporary satisfaction.

Periodically, someone of tremendous stature comes into this world and reveals the nature of God as God truly is—a God nothing whatever like the God most people worship, nothing like the God to whom they pray or about whom they are taught. Whenever such a one comes into this world, he tells of a God that the human race cannot receive, understand, worship, and above all cannot demonstrate. For that reason, the revelation of God has not been a permanent dispensation: it is given to the one, the two, the twelve, the two hundred today, but tomorrow it has all but vanished from the earth.

DEVELOPING SPIRITUAL CONSCIOUSNESS

God is a Spirit and God has to be worshiped in spirit and in truth. Man cannot find God through either a physical or a mental approach; but, in this life, he can develop himself to that place of spiritual consciousness where he can know God, avail himself of God, and live in and of God *now*, not at some future time or after death. That spiritual state of consciousness can be achieved here and now, but to evolve out of the material sense of life requires a change of consciousness which can be attained through the study and practice of specific principles of spiritual living.

The development of an appreciation of music is an example of how such a transformation can occur. A person with no awareness of the nuances of music cannot appreciate or enjoy good music. That does not mean, however, that a person has to die in order to understand music. If the person who at this moment does not enjoy good music or who has no ear for it, that is, no consciousness of it, is able to study under the guidance of a competent and inspired teacher, an appreciation and a love of good music grow, and bit by bit a musical consciousness is developed.

So it is with the things of the Spirit. In a material state of consciousness, there is no love for the things of God: the things of God are foolishness to "man, whose breath is in his nostrils." The things of God do not appeal to the materialist, and even when such a person goes to church to satisfy a member of his family or because of superstition or fear of the future, or for some other reason, that still does not indicate spiritual consciousness.

Spiritual consciousness is developed in much the same way as a consciousness of music is developed. First, there must come a desire for it, and next must come patience and perseverance while seeking and searching for spiritual realization. It takes most of us a long, long time to attain even a slight degree of spiritual appreciation, spiritual realization, or spiritual demonstration, because there are so many by-paths, so many attractions and distractions on the material path of life.

To be spiritually minded is life; to be materially minded is death—the death of the soul, its stagnation during this period of our experience. At some time in our ongoingness, the desire comes for spiritual unfoldment. In some people, this desire is aroused on this plane; some are born into this phase of life with the spiritual hunger in full flower; others die out of this existence without even the knowledge that there is such a thing as the spiritual realm.

In the spiritual life, there is no such thing as time, and in the course of our spiritual ongoing, it will eventually dawn in our consciousness that we have lived forever and that we shall continue to live forever. We can never know how rapidly we are progressing because at a certain stage time ceases. There is a part of us, our Soul, which is deathless and birthless—timeless: It has never been born; It will never die. It is that part of us which was created in the beginning in the image and likeness of God.

INDIVIDUAL REVELATION OF THE NATURE OF GOD

To reveal through spiritual unfoldment that which was never born and which never dies, that which was "in the beginning," is the purpose of The Infinite Way. The most important aspect of spiritual unfoldment as presented through the study of The Infinite Way and the one which always remains the deepest of all subjects is the nature of God. We are told that to know Him aright is life eternal, and to gain that knowledge is our great task.

If we are ignorant of God, it is sinful to delude ourselves into believing that we know something about God and thereby keep our heads buried in the sand. On the other hand, if we really want to be on the God-path, let us not be afraid to admit, "Yes, I have read all these things about God, but I have never met God face to face"; or, "I have been saying all these years that there is no reality to evil and there is no reality to pain, but I do not know whether disease is real or not. All I know is what I have read in books about it, but from my own experience, I do not know." Such an admission leads us to turn within ourselves in sincere humility:

Let me know Thee; let the light of Thy truth illumine my consciousness. Let Thy truth be a lamp unto my feet so that I may live truth and demonstrate it.

Father, intellectually I can accept the truth that because of Thy infinite wisdom and love, sin, disease, and death cannot be real. This I say over and over again, but I cannot demonstrate it. Is there any way in which I can learn the nature of these errors that plague mankind? Is there a way by which I can be dehypnotized so that I am not in eternal fear of dying or of getting old or of being sick or poor?

Such humility is the deepest of prayers, and the answer will always be given to the person who approaches truth in that spirit. It may not come at once, but it will come. Anyone who holds to a path that is consonant with his own inner personal integrity will receive an answer from God. It is only when we try to fool ourselves that we shut out God. I know from actual experience—many, many years of it—that I have only to be honest with myself and turn to God, saying, "Father, I know all the things that are in the books about this, but I am not experiencing it; I do not really know it. Is there a way to guide me to a sure and certain knowledge of it, to lead me into the experience of it, to show me the way of attainment?" It was by working in this way that, step by step, my own unfoldment proceeded.

In pondering the nature of God, eventually it dawned upon me that, if we look around and observe creation in its varied forms, we can catch a glimpse of the nature of God. As we ponder these manifestations of natural phenomena, we are led to the conclusion that there must be an Intelligence operating —an Intelligence greater than that of any man. This understanding will come by actual observance of the myriad forms of creation and by pondering the nature of God as revealed through these forms. As we meditate on the nature of God over a long period of time, we discover things about God of which the human mind has never dreamed, spiritual awareness grows, and we begin to live in and through the Spirit.

GOD SPEAKS THE WORD

The spiritual life can be lived here on earth, and this spiritual life is made possible, in part, through an inner awakening on the subject of the nature of God which in its turn leads to an understanding of the true nature of prayer. Prayer is not asking God for anything; prayer is not petitioning God; prayer is not repeating statements about Him which we hope to make true by our much speaking. Prayer is an actual inner experience which opens consciousness to receive the impartation of the Word. Prayer is what takes place between God and us. It is not a method of reaching God; it is a state of consciousness which enables God to reach us.

How do we arrive at such a place in our study and in our unfoldment? Early in my experience, it became clear to me that prayer must be the word of God. It was through the word of God that all things were established in the beginning: God spoke the Word, and there was day; there was light; there was a universe; there was man. *God* spoke the Word, not man. God spoke the Word, and it happened.

But how many times have we spoken, and nothing has happened? Nothing ever happens when we, as human beings, speak. We ought to be weary of speaking words! We say to the storm, "Cease!" and the thunder and lightning pay no attention to us. They keep right on rolling and flashing. We say to the waves, "Cease!" but the waves roll on—often with accelerated force. We have all spoken words, and nothing has happened. But what happens when God speaks the Word? "Let there be light; and there was light.[1] . . . Rise, take up thy bed, and walk.[2]" And he arose and picked up his bed and walked. Yes, but that does not happen when we speak. It is only when God speaks that it is done.

I learned that when I could be quiet enough inside and could be sufficiently receptive to let God say the Word to me, patients were healed, students were taught, the unemployed found employment, and wondrous things happened in our work, such wondrous things that in the space of a few short years The Infinite Way has spread around the entire world. I did not do that, my word did not do it, and what is more, I do not know any words that can do it; but after many, many years, I have learned how to become still and how to be receptive—how to sit patiently, ever so patiently, until the Word is spoken.

[1] Genesis 1:3.   [2] John 5:8.

With all of man's opaqueness, something always happens when God speaks the Word, even though we do our best to block it because we do not really want God to have His way with us entirely. That might take away from us much of our human good when we are not ready to give it up. Nevertheless, with all the blocks we put in God's way, prayer will ultimately redeem us if we understand that prayer is the word of God that is uttered through us or in us, and that it has nothing to do with any mental process—it has nothing to do with what we know. The very moment we acknowledge: "I know not how to pray. I know not how to go in or come out. I do not know what to pray for," the moment we stop trying to tell God what His business is, in that moment we have gained enough spiritual wisdom to prepare ourselves for the blessing we are seeking.

There is no way for you or me to know what your highest good is or what my highest good is, but this I do know: The word of God is quick and sharp and powerful, and when God speaks the Word, "Let there be light," there is light; and if God says, "Pick up your bed and walk," you pick it up and walk. I know that when the Spirit of God is upon us we are ordained and we can do great spiritual things by virtue of that Spirit. I also know that "where the Spirit of the Lord is, there is liberty."[3]

Neither you nor I, nor anyone else, can create that Spirit of the Lord with affirmations, denials, or statements about It. It cannot be prayed into existence by begging and pleading, although there may be times when we are so mentally disturbed that for a few minutes we will actually turn to God and speak in human language in some such fashion as this: "God, please take over; take hold of me. I am wandering in a wilderness. Hold me." But we are not saying that for the sake of God; that is just a method of getting ourselves out of the way. The

[3] II Corinthians 3:17.

ultimate good is when we are still and quiet enough, sufficiently at peace, to say:

"Speak, Lord; for thy servant heareth."[4] *Thy grace is my sufficiency in all things. I do not ask for food—bread, butter, meat, or wine; I do not ask for clothing, or raiment; I do not ask for success. Thy grace is my sufficiency in all things.*

The miracle of prayer is attaining that state of consciousness, and in that state of consciousness, the Spirit of God can come upon us, the Holy Ghost can descend upon us, the Spirit of the Lord can be present with us, and in that Spirit we find liberty.

As deeper and deeper forms of prayer and meditation are practiced, eventually we arrive at an actual communion with God. Communion is that depth of meditation in which we actually come into the experience of tabernacling with the Spirit of God, and then it is possible to have conversation with God, to receive beautiful and inspiring impartations from God —sometimes in words or thoughts and sometimes as just an awareness of the Presence. There seems to be a flow between God and us—an incoming and an outgoing, a turning and a returning, a sweetness, a gentleness, a peacefulness. Sometimes it transcends all words and thoughts, and eventually the personal sense of self completely disappears, and there is nothing left but God. It is a sense of Self that has no finite or corporeal limitation—a pure state of being.

ATTAINING THE SPIRITUAL KINGDOM

If we are on the spiritual path, we must not be afraid of treading the path alone; we must not be afraid of the ridicule of friends and family; we must not be afraid of lack and limitation. Experiencing a temporary period of lack or limitation or ill health is nothing to be ashamed of or to hide. Such ex-

[4] I Samuel 3:9.

periences merely represent phases of our present development out of which we are working.

Problems are given to us to work out of, and there is no need to hide them. We have not made the claim that we have as yet wholly realized spiritual completeness or that we have achieved our full Christhood. Whatever the nature of our particular problem may be, let us not try to hide it. Let us rather face it and realize that we are on this path for the purpose of realizing our way out of material sense into spiritual consciousness. If we remember that, we shall find that the problem is not nearly as severe or as difficult or as unusual as it seemed at first.

Let us always remember, however, that it is not the function of God to turn a sick body into a well body, or an empty purse into a full purse. Such changes can only be brought about by a change of consciousness. As long as we retain even a measure of material consciousness, that measure must externalize itself, and it can externalize itself in forms of human good as well as human evil. Material sense has no intelligence. It can be a good experience today and a bad one tomorrow, or a bad one today and a good one tomorrow, because it is the nature of material conditions to be sometimes good and sometimes bad.

Whatever measure of material sense, or of what Paul called the carnal mind, remains in us is certain to externalize itself in a carnal condition, and that carnal condition can sometimes be good and sometimes evil. When we rise higher in the understanding of the nature of God and the nature of the error that confronts us, and in proportion as we attain spiritual light, not only will the discords of human existence leave us, but the harmonies of human existence as well.

Everybody seems quite willing to give up the pains, the discords, and the limitations of human experience, but most people cling to human good. They are not ready to exchange their human good even for the kingdom of heaven. Human good is so much better than human evil that we have all come to think of human good as desirable and to want it, not realizing that there are far greater things than man has ever dreamed of: "Eye hath not seen, nor ear heard, neither have entered into the heart of man, the things which God hath prepared for them that love him."[5] No human being can possibly have any idea of the things that God has laid up for those who love Him.

The spiritual universe is not the human universe devoid of error or discord. The spiritual universe is the absence of both human error *and* human good. It is the kingdom of God on earth, not the kingdom of good humanhood or good materiality. It is not the kingdom of more and better matter, but it is a rising above material sense, even good material sense, into spiritual consciousness. As we in The Infinite Way recognize that, we do not become ascetics and reject the human good that comes to us, even though the achievement of human good is not our purpose. Human good comes as "the added things."

There is a spiritual kingdom, an inner kingdom, a kingdom about which mortal man knows nothing. By living and moving and having our being in spiritual awareness, that transformation of our mind, that transformation of consciousness, is wrought which reveals to us the kingdom of heaven on earth.

THE INFINITE NATURE OF INDIVIDUAL BEING

An understanding of the nature of God and the nature of prayer is essential to spiritual unfoldment, but with these must also come a recognition of our true identity. We are not man and we are not effect: we are *I*. The nature of indivdual being is *I*, and *I* is infinite. *I* and the Father are one, and all that the Father has is ours.

Throughout Scripture, we find proof that good flows out *from* our being; it does not flow to our being. Many people are living miserable lives because they are sitting around waiting for love to come to them; others are waiting for friend-

[5] I Corinthians 2:9.

ship to come to them; and still others are waiting for justice and mercy. They wait and wait; they beg and they plead; they even pray, but it does not come. And it never can come. There is only one way in which love, abundance, mercy, justice, and goodness can be demonstrated, and that is to express them— to let them flow out, to cast our bread upon the waters.

Through meditation and then by actual demonstration, I learned that the fullness of the Godhead is within me. God has fulfilled Himself as my individual being, but I can only demonstrate this in proportion to my ability to live it. If I have but a few coins today and am willing to part with one or two of them, sharing them with someone who has still less, or if I have no coins at all but do have an awareness of my identity, and if I am willing to sit and pray and realize that truth for my fellow man—for my friends, for my neighbors, for my enemies—if that is all I have, I cast that bread upon the water. If I can find some way to be a friend, if I can find some way of expressing forgiveness, if I can find some way of being more just and more merciful, if I can accept the Messianic message, "He that hath seen me, hath seen the Father,"[6] and if I begin, in any given moment, to act out that way of life by loving, sharing, forgiving, and co-operating, I have begun the demonstration of my harmony.

Be assured of this: God has not created His own image and likeness and left it lacking for anything. The image and likeness of God, God's own manifestation of Its own being, does not have sufficient money and at the same time insufficient health, or abundant health and not enough money. The image and likeness of that I which I am, the infinite Spirit Itself in individual manifestation and expression, is the embodiment of all that God is. That recognition is a revelation of truth, but it is not the demonstration of truth. Acceptance must be followed by action.

The truth about our own identity, our own inner spiritual

[6] John 14:9.

being, is contrary to all appearances. To appearances, we are aging, dying, sick, sinning human beings. Therefore, it is wise to close our eyes frequently and to realize:

Father, Thou art infinite Being, and that infinite Being is expressed as individual being. I do not claim any such truth for my human identity: I recognize that a human being or a mortal is not divine, but that a human being must die to the sense of self in the realization of the infinite nature of God. I am attempting to "die daily" to my humanhood—not to spiritualize it, but to surrender it in the realization that God is infinite being, that God constitutes individual, spiritual, incorporeal being, invisible being, the being that I am.

"If I make my bed in hell, behold, thou art there."[7] If I mount up to heaven, Thou art there. If "I walk through the valley of the shadow of death,"[8] Thou art there. Why? Because I am there: I am here and I am there, and I am everywhere. I is infinite being. I is Self-completeness.

The whole message of The Infinite Way is a teaching of Self-completeness in God. That does not mean that humanly we are complete or perfect, self-contained or self-maintained. Self-completeness is attained by putting off the human sense of self, surrendering it and acknowledging, "The I of my being can never leave me, nor forsake me. As I was with Abraham, so I am with me. I will never leave me, nor forsake me."

That leads us to that miracle-teaching of Jesus Christ which is an integral part of The Infinite Way:

"I have meat to eat that ye know not of."[9] I am the wine of life; I am the bread of life; I am the resurrection. That I will never leave me nor forsake me. Where I am, I is, for I is the true nature of my being. I is my meat; I is my wine, my water, and my bread. I is the staff of life to me. I is my hiding place. I live and move and have my being in God, in the I that I am.

[7] Psalm 139:8.   [8] Psalm 23:4.   [9] John 4:32.

God is my fortress, and I hide in that fortress which I am. Nothing can in any manner or by any means reach me, assail me, or injure me because I am, and besides me, there are no powers to inflict any injury because I alone is power. I is the resurrection. "I, if I be lifted up from the earth, will draw all men unto me."[10]

Never use the word *I* publicly. It must remain the most sacred and secret word in your entire life-experience. Keep *I* lifted up inside your own being:

How comforting it is to know that I *will never leave me, nor forsake me, to know that* I *is the source of my life, the creative principle of my being.* I *need not look to "man, whose breath is in his nostrils."*[11] *If* I *were lost in the desert or at sea,* I *will be with me and* I *will feed me, sustain me, and bring me safely through. If* I *walk through the valley of the shadow of death,* I *will walk with me and reveal my life eternal unto me.*

I is a secret and sacred prayer. Every time you feel the word *I* inside of you, you are acknowledging that God is closer to you than breathing and nearer than hands or feet. Is there anything closer than *I*? That *I* is the God-power or what we call the Christ, the Spirit of God in man. It is God's individualization of His own being appearing on earth as you. As you voice the word "I" inwardly, secretly and silently open your consciousness in the attitude of "Speak, Lord; for thy servant heareth,"[12] and the Voice you will hear will melt the earth; the voice of the Lord melteth all problems. When that Voice utters Itself in you, the whole earth melts—the earth and all the problems of materialism. Fears will disappear; doubts will vanish; and without thought or planning, events will take place in your experience which could only come to you by divine Grace, by the recognition that *I* in the midst of you is mighty.

[10] John 12:32.   [11] Isaiah 2:22.   [12] I Samuel 3:9.

Let that *I* that you feel have Its way with you. God has planted Himself in the midst of us and, in planting Himself in the midst of us, all things are added unto us. In every seed that is planted in the ground, there is some kind of a power which we call nature that attracts to that seed whatever it needs from the earth. Planted in the midst of us is the presence and power of God, or that which we call the Son of God or the Christ. It is there but for one purpose: to attract to us from out of this world—even from the uttermost ends of the earth—all those things necessary for our development and unfoldment.

If our fulfillment requires that somebody be raised up in North America, Europe, Asia, or Africa, be assured that he will be raised up and brought to our door; or, on the other hand, if it is necessary that we be transported to foreign lands to find that which is requisite for our unfoldment, *I* in the midst of us will transport us wherever it is we need to be. When we believe that our good is dependent upon money, friends, influence, or any human circumstance, we prevent the operation of spiritual law within ourselves, but when we acknowledge that it is not money, influence, or some particular circumstance or set of circumstances that we need, but only the realization of *I*, then we shall find that that realization of *I* will go to the uttermost ends of the earth and draw unto us everything and everybody necessary to our experience.

The basic premise of The Infinite Way is the infinity of individual being, not by virtue of any human event, but by virtue of the divine Grace which has planted *I* in the midst of us. This revelation does not involve improving the human man, but brings to light more and more of the Christ-man which in reality we are. The highest good we know as human beings is to be better human beings, healthier human beings, wealthier human beings, or greater human beings; but there comes a point in spiritual realization when we know that even if we could become the healthiest or the wealthiest human beings in all the world, that would not be the solution to life's problems. Only *I* within us—*I* in the midst of us—enables us to rest in spiritual peace.

Bind the word *I* on your forehead; bind It on your arm; post It on the gate of your house. "Pray without ceasing";[13] keep these words of truth within you and keep making yourself receptive until this Word takes root. Then after it has taken root, wait patiently for It to bud and blossom and give you Its fruitage.

ACROSS THE DESK

Sooner or later there arises in each of us a longing to be one with our divine nature, an intense hunger for the true meat and a thirst for the spiritual water and wine, but we do not recognize what is happening and we incorrectly interpret this Soul-longing as pain, lack, frustration, and unhappiness.

In the Song of Solomon, the desire for union with God is interpreted as a human longing for the presence of a loved one. In mystical writings, we meet with those who have wandered the whole world over seeking happiness or peace, and with sinners seeking solace by satisfying the desires of the senses. So, I have seen the sick, reaching for either medicine or prayers—for material pills or mental powers—not realizing the depth of their own longing for God. Once they awaken to their real need which is to know Him aright, to be reunited with the fount of Life from which they spring, they will be on the spiritual path which leads to freedom.

In the midst of any trial or tribulation, try to understand that God is seeking you to bring you back home to Him, not in death but in life eternal. Realize that this very pain, unhappiness, or lack is but that sense of separation from God and immediately rest back in the assurance of His presence. Relax and let His hand steal into yours. Let His grace be a benediction unto you.

[13] I Thessalonians 5:17.

CHAPTER X

THE GOVERNMENT IS ON
HIS SHOULDERS

Once again the world is in one of its periodic crises—one of the many hundreds that have occurred at intervals throughout history. If you are any student at all of world affairs, even to the extent of just reading the front pages of the newspapers or hearing news broadcasts, you must be aware of the fact that there are at least a half dozen major problems facing the world, any one of which could result in the end of this particular civilization and for which no one has offered any kind of solution.

We are facing world conditions that are insurmountable humanly. They are not really insurmountable, however, because there are no problems that ever can arise that cannot be settled; and when I say settled, I do not mean settled on the basis of expediency or compromise, but settled advantageously for all concerned. An analogy can be drawn between periods in world history and periods in our individual experience. For example, sometimes there are physical disorders that can be healed easily and inexpensively through medical aid, and as long as our physical ills are on that level, there is nothing much for us to worry about. A few cents' worth of aspirin here or a few cents' worth of bicarbonate of soda there or a few dollars' worth of surgery, and we are all right. It is only when the doctor tells us that we have an incurable disease that we feel we are up against a humanly insurmountable problem, and then it is that many people are driven to find a spiritual solution.

So it is in world affairs. As long as the world was going along in what may be called "the good old days," there were very few problems for which a solution could not be found because they were usually localized in some particular area. But the solution to these problems was only a superficial one, and the basic issues were never completely resolved. When, however, these tensions and conflicts became world-wide in scope and a spark in one part of the globe kindled a fire whose devastating flames swept almost instantaneously around the entire world, we were then faced with a really deadly and incurable disease from the human standpoint.

Whether it is another world war or economic disaster which could plunge the globe into chaos, so far as the human picture is concerned, the world situation is critical. The greatest danger, however, does not lie in losing our life or our possessions, but in losing our Soul. In fact, the loss of our physical sense of life is the least thing we have to fear. What we have to concern ourselves with is the danger to the Soul, for when man is enslaved, he has lost his Soul temporarily—he no longer dare call it his own. Therefore, a danger to freedom is a far greater danger than the loss of physical life. That is why I repeat that these are critical days for the world.

The nations of the world, as such, are not seeking spiritual light or spiritual existence. They are seeking a cessation of war and that not so much that peace may be established as for their own individual welfare. Let us not forget that the United States was not concerned about the hundreds of thousands who were wiped out at one blow by an atomic bomb. Their excuse for throwing it was, "We saved tens of thousands of lives of our own soldiers." Yes, but we took hundreds of thousands of lives of some other nation. Our attitude was one of "What has that to do with us? We saved our own lives."

It is the same with every nation. The nation that first used a weapon superior to that of its enemies did not consider its opponent: it concerned itself only with ending the war for its own benefit.

Never believe for a moment that you or I can make the world's demonstration for it. The reliances upon which the people of the world have depended cannot be taken away from them at their present state of consciousness because if these props are removed, we have taken away their God. The world has to resolve its conflicts and settle its problems in its own way and in accord with its present development of consciousness.

Do you remember how Peter tried to walk on the water and how the Master had to rescue him? No one can walk on the water for anyone else. Each one has to learn for himself. In other words, the spiritual identity of every one of us has to be awakened so that we can realize our true identity and demonstrate it.

OUR FUNCTION IN THE WORLD CRISIS

Let us not for a moment think that we can take a spiritual stand for the world and make its demonstration. Our prayer is not that the world follow some predetermined course of action which we have decided is the right one, but that material sense be destroyed in order that brotherly love may be established in the hearts and souls and minds of peoples and governments all over the world.

In political life, it must certainly be recognized that there is a great deficiency of spiritual love. Politicians who occupy positions of great power and apparently hold the fate of millions in their grasp speak eloquently about the spiritual principles upon which our nation was founded, but instead of taking a firm stand for a course of action which would preserve those principles and be in the best interests of the country, they usually count the number of votes involved and then act from the standpoint of expediency.

Spiritual students, on the other hand, understand that man shall not live by bread alone—not dollars alone, nor votes alone—but by every word that proceedeth out of the mouth of God. In the secrecy and sanctity of our homes, you and I can take this spiritual stand. Our attitude is that there be neither good humanhood nor bad humanhood, but that the activity of the Christ destroy material sense and be released into human consciousness to introduce the reign of love—*My kingdom*—not that which is humanly right or humanly wrong, but the spiritual kingdom.

All over the world there are dedicated students who at least three times a day are turning within for a realization of the Christ to dispel material sense in human consciousness, whether that human consciousness is north or south, east or west, occidental or oriental. Through such meditation, there is the possibility of influencing events all over this world—not by praying for your side or for my side, but by dedicating ourselves to the realization of the activity of the Christ, dispelling and destroying material sense and revealing the spiritual kingdom on earth as it is in heaven.

Then we shall find that here and there public officials, without knowing why, are responding to the spiritual impulse and are becoming the avenue through which greater good flows into the world. Behind the scenes, there is a spiritual power operating, impelling men to do things contrary even to their own best vote-getting interests, and eventually through the activity of that impersonal power, we shall witness the kingdom of God established on earth.

So far as the world is concerned, it must continue to work out its problems in whatever way it seems led, but our function is to be that spiritual underground which is praying continuously that material sense be destroyed, that "Thy kingdom come on earth as it is in heaven." Every person has the right to demonstrate his own state of consciousness: the world has the right to live according to its, although we continue to pray that that state of consciousness be lifted up to Christ-con-sciousness.

Have you ever stopped to realize that the activity of the Christ must have a human being through whom to operate? Have you ever stopped to realize that nothing is taking place except what is taking place in consciousness? If we are func-tioning negatively, negative things are happening; but if we are functioning spiritually, spiritual things.

It took an individual, lifting himself above religious super-stition to an actual experience of God within, to lead the Hebrews out of slavery. Then later, it was Christ Jesus who took people out from under the law and lifted them up into Grace. He was the instrument through whom the Christ worked to dispel sin, disease, and poverty. Thirty years later, Paul was raised up to go out and carry the message of the Christ into the world. There is no functioning of the Christ without a human being through whom It can operate.

The Christ has to function through your consciousness or my consciousness if our family, community, or nation is to be benefited. Each of us is a tiny little thread in the world's scheme, a strand in this great spiritual rope. Most of us begin equally as nonentities, and whatever measure of success we have is due to the measure in which we open ourselves to the activity of the Christ. We cannot wait for somebody else to do it. We have to accept our responsibility because if the Christ is to be loosed into the world to bring healing and regenera-tion, each one of us has to be an instrument for that Christ-activity.

We are either thinking destructively or spiritually, or not at all. If we permit ourselves to be filled with the Spirit of God —even if in the beginning it is only with the letter of truth—

one day we shall know as did the Master, "The Spirit of the Lord is upon me, because he hath anointed me to preach the gospel to the poor; he hath sent me to heal the brokenhearted, to preach deliverance to the captives, and recovering of sight to the blind, to set at liberty them that are bruised."[1]

There is no use indulging in vain hopes that God is going to enter this world and stop wars, depressions, or overcome labor troubles. God enters the world and operates only through human consciousness. There has to be a consciousness through which God can function.

The more dedicated an individual is to truth, the greater degree of spiritual awareness he attains and the greater the fruitage in the form of healings and harmony, and ultimately the greater influence he is in his community, nation, and the world at large. Those who can rise to the heights of an Abraham, Isaac, a Jacob, Moses, an Isaiah, a Jesus, or a John will do the great works of the world. Each one sets his own limits because it is the degree of his dedication that determines the fruitage. The activity of the Christ can free the entire world from limitation of every nature—poverty, sin, disease, and death— but the Christ cannot do such things unless It has instruments through which to work.

God is, but in and of itself that is of no use to the world. Christ is, but that too is of no use to the world. Only when the power of God is centered in and through individual consciousness does it make its appearance on earth for the benefit of the world.

WORLD PROBLEMS WILL BE SOLVED BY A CHANGE OF CONSCIOUSNESS

Ultimately, the peace which has already been established in consciousness will be manifest on earth—and I do not mean a cessation of war—I mean peace, real peace, lasting peace. According to the record of history, there have been only two

[1] Luke 4:18.

major reasons for war—religion and economics—and both of these causes can be eliminated. The religious wars will cease when all men are willing to admit and recognize that there is only one God. Then religion will never again serve the purpose of hate, bigotry, or animosities because if there is only one God, we are all children of God and we are brothers in that spiritual household.

In the same way when, as is now already taking place, nations can sit down together at the conference table and discuss business constructively rather than conniving to capture world markets at any cost, there will be an end to commercial rivalry, and the world will witness a new era of co-operation. These commercial differences will always exist unless, and until, nations can sit down together and work out their respective economic problems in the climate of sanity, intelligence, and justice. This is beginning to take place, and it represents that change of consciousness on the part of men which is basic to enduring peace.

When there is a change in human consciousness from self-seeking and obdurately insisting upon our personal and national will, wanting only the success of our own army and industry, then we will begin to move forward on the spiritual path. The progress that has been made thus far is because there are men and women praying, not praying for their side —for their armies or nations—but praying that God's kingdom be established in human consciousness in every quarter of the earth.

Our individual consciousness is important to the safety and security and the peace of this world. In the degree that our consciousness holds within it no animosity, bigotry, hate, or jealousy and is willing for the enemy as well as the friend to prosper, it becomes a center for the activity of the Christ.

If we continue living our human lives only for ourselves or our families, we perpetuate the evils of the world. If we permit our minds to be filled only with human thoughts, human

desires, and human ambitions, we block and keep out the
Christ from our community, nation, and world. Again let me
remind you of this great truth: *The Christ has entrance into
the world only through human consciousness,* and It raises
up those of spiritual enlightenment.

The words of the Christ have been on earth for thousands
of years, and they have never passed completely from consciousness. In fact, Jesus told us that they would never die, and
they never will. In every generation and in every age, God has
raised up somebody to keep the Word alive, and God will continue to do so until enough people respond and make themselves
individually responsible so that their consciousness becomes an
avenue for the Christ.

Let us accept the responsibility that our consciousness is
either being a blank to the world, being destructive to the
world, or being spiritually constructive. We determine that by
the degree to which we open ourselves to spiritual truth. The
conscious devotion of a few minutes of every hour to truth
keeps our consciousness filled with truth continuously.

It would be helpful to the world if all of us who read
this chapter would participate in periods of meditation in which
we do not concern ourselves with our own health or wealth
or that of our family or nation, but in which our sole function
is to realize the presence and power of the Christ. When we
have felt that Presence, the Christ is loosed into the world,
thereby destroying material sense and establishing the kingdom
of God on earth. Our consciousness is this activity of the Christ,
so therefore, we will patiently wait for that feeling of the
Presence, sitting in quietness and peace until it is released.

It is said in Scripture that if there are ten righteous men
in the city, the city will be saved. The very moment that we
release mankind from condemnation, we help release this world
from fear. As we realize the true nature of individual being
and release every individual from condemnation in the realization of God as his true being, every individual within our orbit

is released into God. Thus war becomes an impossibility. True, there will always be differences of opinion, for we are all at different states and stages of consciousness, and each one is entitled to his own opinions and to his own unfoldment.

APPLYING THE PRINCIPLE OF IMPERSONAL HEALING TO WORLD AFFAIRS

Those who have had healings through metaphysical or spiritual means have witnessed the nullifying of error in one form or another, but how many of us have any knowledge as to how the error was eradicated and nullified?

Here is the principle: Any form of discord that touches our experience is not our fault. It is not even our fault if we sin or do not sin. I know that there are some self-righteous people who really believe that it is possible to be good, but that is because they are living in an ivory tower. They would be shocked, however, at how quickly they would be pulled out of that tower if a temptation to which they were vulnerable raised its head. Then they would learn how impossible it is to be good of oneself. It is only in the degree that we understand that sickness, sin, lack, or any discord is the product of universal error, not individual error, but the universal misunderstanding of truth or lack of understanding of truth, that we free ourselves and others from any condemnation.

The very first thing a practitioner has to do when a patient asks for help is to give up any sense of judgment, criticism, or condemnation of the person. Any such sense would be personalizing error, and it would fasten it to the patient instead of freeing him from it. As soon as the practitioner realizes that this is not the patient's sin, not his disease, his lack, or his belief, but that this is a universal hypnotism or appearance of which he is an innocent victim, the patient begins to experience his freedom; the weight of guilt is lifted from him, and very soon the entire condition dissolves.

When we come to a place of absolutely impersonal healing,

where we do not take the patient into our treatment at all but where we deal entirely with universal belief, we will then begin to perceive how this important healing principle of The Infinite Way can be applied to the solution of world problems.

World problems will be solved by nullifying material sense because the problems of every nation are the result of material sense. No nation on earth is working solely from the standpoint either of the freedom of mankind or of the prosperity of mankind except as it may be attained without any loss to itself.

Therefore, although there are some nations that in a measure are working humanly for the good of mankind and without ulterior motives, this is not the solution to world problems any more than human betterment is the solution to individual health or supply. The principle that will solve individual problems will ultimately solve world problems, and that principle is the realization that we are not dealing with good people or with bad people: we are dealing with the carnal mind, the belief in two powers.

As soon as we recognize that error is not personal to the patient, and transfer it to the carnal mind, the patient is well on the way to experiencing a healing. So it is with world affairs. Let us stop praising or condemning governments and nations and begin to work with the impersonal Christ in the realization that all the error that has ever existed, or does exist, is the carnal mind, and then realize that the carnal mind is not and never has been power. It is only operative in human consciousness because it has been accepted as power.

THE ULTIMATE SOLUTION WILL BE FOUND
IN SPIRITUAL POWER

Many times the question is asked, "Will not spiritual power heal the world?" And the answer is, "Yes, but it must be understood what spiritual power is and how it is to be employed." People have been praying to God to remove sin, heal disease, and bring peace on earth for thousands of years and yet, up to this time, sin, disease, and war have not been eliminated.

Spiritual power is the way, but spiritual power is not a power that destroys evil. People have been trying to use this power to overcome sin, disease, and death, but they have failed miserably and will continue to fail until they come to the realization that spiritual power is not a power that can be used. If we could use it, we would be master of it, and that we are not. But we can let spiritual power be our master; we can let spiritual power govern us; we can let spiritual power govern our body, health, and supply by not trying to use it, but by relaxing every effort of our mind, learning to be still and letting spiritual power *be* the power. In the presence of such power, error quickly dissolves. Therein is the great secret. Spiritual power cannot be used, and praying to God to do something does not generate spiritual power.

Spiritual power is the salvation of the world. To prove it, we have to demonstrate in our personal experience that there is a Power and that this Power releases us from the carnal mind and any of its effects, any of its beliefs, or any of its forms. How? By relaxing and giving up mental effort, giving up mental strife against any particular form of sin, fear, or disease. Yes, we should even have the courage to tell fear to eat us up if it can. If it has so much power, why not let it demonstrate it? If our fear is going to do anything to us, why not let it do it now? It will eventually, if it has that much power. What we shall find, however, is that fear is not power—it is only power as long as we fight it.

When we use, or attempt to use, spiritual power, we have ensured defeat at the outset, but if we release ourselves to spiritual power, we shall find what the Psalmist found, that the Lord is our shepherd and that He does set a table in the wilderness; the Lord does lead us beside the still waters and into green pastures. That is what we find when we give up the struggle against error.

World history is full of names like Pharaoh, Pilate, Caesar, Judas Iscariot, the Kaiser, Hitler, Stalin, and many more. And the world will continue to be overrun with dictators and tyrants until somebody comes along who realizes that the influence of such people is not removed from the world by doing away with them or by defeating their armies. As soon as one powerful leader is defeated, another springs up who represents that same evil, perhaps in an even more vicious form.

The answer does not lie in fighting fire with fire; the answer does not lie in fighting disease with more disease. The solution to the subject of health is to realize first of all that disease is a condition of the carnal mind, or whatever term is used to mean the universal belief or universal hypnotism of human-hood which had its beginning in the belief in two powers. That is the origin of the carnal mind. If there were no belief in good and evil, there would be no carnal mind. In proportion as an individual attains the consciousness that does not give power to good or evil, in that degree has that individual risen above the human mind and its woes.

The solution comes from knowing the truth and then abiding in the Word. First, we must know the truth that all forms of error represent but the "arm of flesh," the carnal mind, universal belief, nothingness, and then rest in that Word. We must not battle, and above all, we must not believe that one condition is good and another condition is evil. World conditions should never be approached from the standpoint that one side is right and one wrong. Healing is brought about when we drop all sense of right and wrong, and come to the point where we realize, "God's will be done, not man's." Then the solution will come to the surface.

All affairs of the world can ultimately be settled in this way, but only in the degree that we first settle our individual minor affairs, and thereby demonstrate that we have discovered the nature of spiritual power. Spiritual power is the secret of health, supply, and peace in our relationships, but spiritual power is not a power that we can use. It is a power that we let use us.

SPIRITUAL PRINCIPLES IN WORLD AFFAIRS

The principles of spiritual healing are effective not only in the healing of disease and the regeneration of the individual —in his morals, finances, and human characteristics—but they go further afield than that. They work in business and professional life and in political and governmental affairs. They work wherever they are applied seriously, sacredly, secretly, and unselfishly. They will not work, however, if anything of a selfish nature is the motivating force. In other words, they will not work if we are trying to elect a specific candidate to office or if we are trying to secure a specific job for a certain person. These principles will not be effective if there is any trace of selfishness, self-profit, or anything of a personal nature because these are universal principles of good, and they operate on an impersonal basis.

The only reason that bad government exists is because of the belief in two powers—the acceptance of the carnal mind. But are there two powers? No, God constitutes individual being; God is the very nature of man; and therefore, man's nature is godly and good, and these qualities of evil—ambition, lust, greed, stupidity, ignorance, and fear—are the carnal mind. But there is no carnal mind, for there is no mind but the one. Therefore, these qualities have no channel or avenue of operation and no law to support them. They constitute the "arm of flesh" or nothingness.

And the government shall be upon his shoulder: and . . . of the increase of his government and peace there shall be no end.

Isaiah 9:6,7

OUR PRIVILEGE AND DUTY

Right now, nothing is more important for Infinite Way students than daily prayer on the subject of international relations.

Our students can be neither Republicans, Democrats, Socialists, nor Communists. We are functioning spiritually, and our realization is that *all* government is on His shoulders—never at the mercy of man. Our daily realization is that the carnal mind is impersonal and has no person through whom to act as an instrument or means of action. God constitutes the government on earth as in heaven, and the belief in two powers is nullified as we understand its operation to be devoid of spiritual life or law.

ACROSS THE DESK

I hope that you who are students of The Infinite Way are not touched by the news of the day, for surely you have learned by now that the press, radio, and television report only what has already passed into history.

These media of communication are not yet equipped to handle the real news of the hidden and underlying forces which manipulate the events which form the news. What appears in print or is heard on the air is but the consequence of the invisible forces which produced events leading up to today's news reports.

Let me illustrate. Several years ago, I wrote that students of The Infinite Way should disregard the ominous international news because peace had already taken place. This peace to which I referred really was an activity in the Invisible, and the first fruitage evident was a faint but distinct spiritual awakening. Even though it is a tangible experience in consciousness, the press cannot report this spiritual awakening because it is not yet visible in form.

As this awakening takes form, people all over the world seek spiritual knowledge, an understanding of spiritual principles, and the experience of spiritual living. Thus, human consciousness around the globe is being molded, establishing the invisible peace in men's consciousness. This is all occurring on the invisible plane, but the press can only report the *effects* of this spiritual awakening, as the "old man" is rapidly being "put off" and the "new man" of the Spirit is being born.

The newspapers of tomorrow will report that world peace is established on earth, but world peace is actually already established, although not yet ready for recognition and announcement by the press.

Be not concerned with what you see and hear, but look deeply and note the signs of the spiritual awakening now beginning to take visible form. Note the call from all over the world for greater spiritual light and understanding and rejoice that "My kingdom" is now come and soon will be seen and recognized on earth.

CHAPTER XI

WHAT HAVE YOU IN THE HOUSE?

Every day of our lives, in some form or other, we meet with the same problem which the poor widow faced when Elijah said, "Bring me, I pray thee, a morsel of bread," and perhaps we may feel just as destitute as did she. Fortunately for her, she had enough spiritual intuition to understand his request; and so when she answered that she had "but an handful of meal in a barrel, and a little oil in a cruse," the great Hebrew master told her to make him a little cake first because "the barrel of meal shall not waste, neither shall the cruse of oil fail."[1] She obeyed. She took her cruse of oil with its few drops and began to pour, and it never ran dry because to the few drops that she had were added more and more.

Jesus used this same principle in multiplying the loaves and fishes. When there were multitudes to be fed and Jesus commanded his disciples, "Give ye them to eat," and when they demurred that they had only five loaves and two fishes, "he took the five loaves and the two fishes, and looking up to heaven, he blessed them, and brake, and gave to the disciples to set before the multitude."[2] Those five loaves and fishes were

[1] I Kings 17:11, 12, 14.   [2] Luke 9:13, 16.

a sufficiency for the whole multitude, with twelve baskets full left over.

The principle involved in these two examples of supply is this: You are infinite; all that God is, you are, and all that the Father has is yours. Do not begin searching in your pocketbook to see if you can prove this, because we are not interested at this moment in what the world calls sensible evidence: we are interested in a principle of life.

BEGIN TO POUR

Because of the infinite nature of your being, you have one hundred per cent integrity even if at this moment you are not expressing all of it. You have all the loyalty, fidelity, and benevolence which emanate from God; you have all of God's life which is immortal, all of God's Soul which is purity. You have the very Spirit of God in you—all of it, not just a part of it, for you cannot divide Spirit, you cannot divide Soul.

No spiritual quality can be divided—you either have all of it or none, and to have none is impossible because of *Omnipresence*. There is only All-Presence. All of God is yours now; all that the Father has is yours now: the life of God is yours; the mind of God is yours; the Soul of God is yours.

Begin with that principle as a foundation, and then begin "to pour," begin "to break." You embody within yourself the infinity of God. All that the Father has and is, is within you —all of it. You are not dependent upon a government, upon a husband, a wife, or a job, even though at this present time, one of these might seem to be the source of your supply. Therefore, do not cast these aside, but begin right now to break your dependence on them by understanding that you have within you the source of your good. Not even God can send it to you because it is incorporated within you from the beginning. "Before Abraham was, I am"[3] in you in the fullness.

[3] John 8:58.

In the practical demonstration of this principle, you must begin with this moment to find ways to pour from your cruse of oil, "to break" your particular loaves and fishes. For example, if you are struggling with a sense of ill health, instead of trying to acquire health, you must begin to recognize, "I embody my health; and therefore, it must pour out from the center of my being. I will not seek to gain health, but to express the health which is my divine right."

If you are struggling with a sense of lack or limitation, you must begin to pour. If necessary, take a few pennies every day and give them away to somebody who can make use of them, but begin to get them into circulation, instead of waiting for more pennies to come in. Do not be reckless and give more than you have; do not run up a charge account and trust God to meet it next month. First provide the money needed this month out of the infinity of your being, and then go and spend it next month. Demonstrate it first and spend it next. Do not spend it first and trust God next. Do your trusting first.

It is possible that you have dammed up inside of you the very thing that you want. Probably most of you would like to be forgiven for some act of omission or commission in your life, and the way to gain that forgiveness is to forgive. Begin to forgive all those who have despitefully used you, all those who have persecuted and wronged you. Begin to forgive all the dictators and tyrants of the world who have been a direct or indirect cause of suffering in your experience. Begin to forgive those members of your family who are not appreciative of what you do for them. Begin right now to ask that they never be punished for their sins. Our prayer should be, "Father, I pray that they may be forgiven their sins without paying any penalty. I have committed a few sins myself that I would like to have forgiven without my paying any penalty. Let everyone be forgiven."

It may be that you would like to gain recognition from certain people or from the world, but there is only one way to get it: give recognition to those people you know deserve recognition.

Many people ask for help to gain companionship, but actually what they want is a companion, not companionship. If they wanted companionship, they would go out and express it, because everyone has companionship within himself—nobody ever has been devoid of companionship. It is a quality of being, and it cannot come to anyone—it has to flow out from him. So if you were on a desert island and there was not even a man Friday with whom to companion, you could go down to the water's edge and companion with the fishes or the pebbles on the beach or the birds in the air. In some way or other, you must begin to express companionship, and then you will find that you will have more companionship in your life than you can find time to enjoy.

INFINITY IS THE MEASURE OF YOUR CAPACITY

Sometimes people who do not know me think that I am theorizing when I talk this way or that I am teaching unproved principles, but everything that I say to you I have had to prove. I have had to be at death's door twice, and come back, so that I could learn and teach the principles of healing. I have been in the position where I was very grateful that at one time some restaurants served orange juice and two doughnuts for ten cents for breakfast, because that was the measure of my financial capacity at that moment, and there were many, many days when that breakfast represented my full day's meal unless somebody invited me out for another one. I have had to demonstrate supply; I have had to demonstrate health; I have had to demonstrate companionship.

Early in my spiritual experience, I came to realize the importance of helping to support the spiritual work of the world. I had to demonstrate that I could put a dollar in the collection plate every Sunday, even when I did not know where that dollar was coming from, but I knew that it was God's responsibility to see that I had it. By agreeing in advance that it would be there, it was there, so that in a few weeks I found myself ashamed to limit my contribution to a dollar and began to increase it to two dollars, then to three, and later to five because, when I began to pour, God poured out His infinite supply so abundantly to me.

Be assured of this: You are infinite. God is the measure of your capacity—physically, mentally, financially, morally, and spiritually. *God is the measure of your capacity.* Even though you may not be able to demonstrate the fullness of God's power because it does not lie within your capacity or mine to prove that fullness yet, the fullness is there.

Do not be concerned whether or not you can buy a yacht or a private plane, but ask yourself, "Can I take a few pennies every day and secretly send them out where they will do someone some good?" Always remember that what alms you do must be done in secret. Always remember to retire every day into a quiet corner, and ask yourself this question, "What have I in the house today?"

Today it may be a quarter; tomorrow it may be a little more love or a little more patience, kindness, tolerance, or forgiveness. Every day it will be something different; and, therefore, if you embark on the spiritual path, you must ask yourself this question every day because every day will make its particular demands upon you, and these you must fulfill. So be prepared to pour. Discipline yourself so that you never expect good to come to you, but always expect it to flow out from you.

LOOK ONLY TO GOD

In the same way, do not look to anyone for gratitude; do not look to anyone for appreciation; do not look to anyone for reward because those things must come to you from God, not from man. You will be surprised what a difference it makes in your home when you no longer expect anything from your husband, your wife, or your children, but steadfastly let your expectancy be from God and then are willing to pour it out and share it with those of your household without asking for reward, gratitude, or appreciation.

Applying this same principle to your business activities, you will be surprised at how quickly promotion and recognition in a monetary form will come to you when you give of your God-qualities without expecting reward, recognition, or anything else. That is because your heavenly Father which seeth in secret rewards you openly. Your reward must come from God and not from man.

It is true that your reward may seem to come *through* man. For example, for those of us who are actively engaged in the healing practice, students and patients will express their gratitude to us in tangible form, but no practitioner or teacher dare look to his patients or his students for it. Only when he looks to God for these things, do his patients or students receive the God-impulse which impels them to be grateful, to share, and to be loving. It is not inherent in human nature to be any of those things. Human nature is always grasping, always on the seeking end, looking for what it can get; human nature wants to get and get endlessly: spiritual nature always wants to pour out.

Every one of you has an eternal relationship with God— a relationship of oneness. If your life is lived daily and hourly in that relationship, with a continuous realization that your awareness of God brings forth everything necessary to your experience, you need never look to any human being for your good.

Begin now to enter into that personal relationship with God if you have not already done so. Make it a matter of daily acknowledgment:

"I and my Father are one,"[4] *and so I turn to the Father every hour of every day, realizing that the Father is always with me*

[4] John 10:30.

—the divine Presence is always within me. That I within never leaves me, nor forsakes me.

When you do that, you will find your good flowing forth abundantly, not *to* you, but *from* you, and yet, in the outer picture, it will appear to be coming to you. You can prove the truth of this principle because all you have to do is to dam it up for just a little while by stopping the outflow, and then watch how quickly the inflow stops also.

THE ACTIVITY OF TRUTH IN CONSCIOUSNESS IS THE SECRET OF HARMONY

The secret of the Bible can be summed up in the one question: "What have you in your house?" If your answer is, "I have all the Godhead bodily; I have all the dominion of God; I have the joy of God, the peace of God; I have the security and safety of God; I have the supply of God," you will find it appearing in tangible form in the external world. To try to get the supply of anything out here is futile because there is nothing out here except time and space. Whatever you demonstrate has to come as an evolution from within your own being, as an outpicturing of what you have in your consciousness.

There is no use trying to demonstrate anything outside your own being. Turn within and demonstrate what you already have in the house. If you have a consciousness of God as supply and a consciousness of God as the source of all beauty, intelligence, wisdom, guidance, and protection, that is all you will ever need. Then you can walk around this entire world with nothing but the clothes on your back, and yet always find that wherever you are, there is everything necessary. You carry it with you.

BEGIN TO EXPRESS YOUR INFINITY BY SHARING

Hundreds of years ago Shakespeare wrote:

> My bounty is as boundless as the sea,
> My love as deep; the more I give to thee
> The more I have, for both are infinite.

When you begin to draw upon your God-bounty, your God-supply, your God-love, do you not see how infinite it is? If, then, you have an infinite bounty and an infinite love, can any more be added to you? Can you add to infinity?

There is no way to get: whatever comes must come from within. You must draw on your bounty; you must draw on your love, which is infinite. Let it flow out and never seek to have it come to you. That makes of life a giving, not a getting, accomplishing, or achieving.

Thousands of years ago, the Hebrews made the discovery that their firstfruits must be given to God:

Honour the Lord with thy substance, and with the firstfruits of all thine increase:
So shall thy barns be filled with plenty, and thy presses shall burst out with new wine.

PROVERBS 3:9,10

Their way of giving of their firstfruits was to give ten per cent of their crops, their cattle, their gold, or whatever they had to the church. You can do the same thing today by setting aside some portion of your income—whatever percentage you decide upon as right for you—and then giving it to any spiritual, benevolent, or impersonal purpose which seems worthy to you.

The percentage or specific amount is not as important as adhering to the principle of giving your firstfruits to God, even to the extent of doing without in order to practice this principle. That sets up a pattern of giving based on your realization that your bounty is infinite because it is God's bounty, not yours personally. Then you are not afraid to part with any of it as your firstfruits.

During the Second World War, some of the parents who had children going into the armed forces asked me to care for their children while they were in the service, that is, to take up daily work for their safety and security. In each case, my reply was, "No, I cannot do this unless your son or daughter desires it, and then only if he or she is willing to co-operate with me."

At first, some parents thought that was being very hardhearted, but it was only being honest. I have no special influence with God which enables me to promise safety or security to certain favored individuals. There is, however, a principle of life that will be the safety and security of anybody who is willing to pay the price of safety and security.

What I demanded of these young men and women was their firstfruits. They had to promise me that when they awakened in the morning they would pray for their enemy—not for themselves, not for their allies, and not for their families back home. They were to give the firstfruits to God by saying a prayer for the enemy. After that, they were free to do any kind of praying for anybody else the rest of the day. Anyone who will open his eyes in the morning and pray for the enemy has given the firstfruits to God because the Master reveals that the only effective prayer is to pray for one's enemies.

Let your life be a life of givingness—giving out of the infinity which you are. Give your first prayer to your enemy. Give the first of your supply to God for any spiritual purpose that you wish. Give love out of the infinity of love within you.

Life consists of giving—but not merely out of a bank account. Give out of the infinite boundless supply of God.

Christhood never seeks to receive. There is no record in the entire New Testament of the Master's seeking health, wealth, recognition, reward, fame, payment, or gratitude. The Christ shines; Its complete activity is that of shining. That is why the Christ is often referred to as the light. Light cannot receive anything: Light is a flowing; light is an expression; light is an outpouring. So is Christhood. It never has any desire to receive anything; It is Itself the infinity of God in individual expression. . . .

The principle of abundance is: "*To him that hath, shall be given.*" Practice this principle by casting your bread upon the waters, giving freely of yourself and your possessions, knowing that what you are giving is God's, and that you are merely the instrument as which it flows out into the world. Never look for a return, but rest in quiet confidence in the assurance that within is the fountain of life, and *His* grace *is* your sufficiency in all things. In that certainty, born of an inner understanding of the letter of truth, you *have*. The cup of joy runs over, and all that the Father has flows forth into expression.[5]

ACROSS THE DESK

At one time it looked as if the United States were being gripped in the clutches of fear. There seemed to be a whole philosophy of fear fed through the many avenues of communication.

Fear knows no boundaries, and so across the sea the cloud sped rapidly until, first, prosperity gave us the fear and chills of inflation; and quickly there followed the fever of the fear of depression and deflation. *Fear must always have a form.* Always there must be *something* to fear, or there would be no fear.

But fear is alien to Americans and could not possibly take deep root in the soil of our consciousness. America is a nation of pioneers. Americans have inherited the qualities of every known race of courageous men and women who have traveled across mountains and seas to reach this nation's shores, ancestors who fought ancient tyrannies to find freedom of mind and body in the healthy atmosphere of a new land. Countless Americans are descendants of those who dared the mountains, streams, and storms to build a new life in a new land.

There is no fear in our Soul, our mind, or in our body. As a nation, America has already overcome all that ever could be feared. There is no soil in American consciousness in which fear can take root. There is no alien thought or thing in our national,

[5] Joel S. Goldsmith, *Practicing the Presence* (New York: Harper & Brothers, 1958), pp. 89-92.

racial, or religious life that has not already been overcome. There is nothing left to fear.

Fear thou not; for I am with thee: be not dismayed; for I am thy God: I will strengthen thee; yea, I will help thee; yea, I will uphold thee with the right hand of my righteousness.

Behold, all they that were incensed against thee shall be ashamed and confounded: they shall be as nothing; and they that strive with thee shall perish.

Thou shalt seek them, and shalt not find them, even them that contended with thee: they that war against thee shall be as nothing, and as a thing of nought.

For I the Lord thy God will hold thy right hand, saying unto thee, Fear not; I will help thee.   ISAIAH 41:10-13

Be strong and of a good courage; be not afraid, neither be thou dismayed: for the Lord thy God is with thee whithersoever thou goest.   JOSHUA 1:9

CHAPTER XII

THE PRINCIPLE OF NONPOWER

Christmas holidays hold many important lessons for us, and it would be well to approach this season with an understanding of the nature of all our holidays, or holy days, as symbolizing important aspects of the spiritual life.

In ancient times when truth was taught only to those who had some measure of education—and usually this meant only to those in the upper stratum of society—in order to keep these teachings from the uneducated masses who might, in their ignorance, misunderstand and misapply them, all teaching was done by symbols. That the Master recognized this fact and the desirability of giving the most sacred teachings only to the few is evidenced by his cautioning his followers against casting pearls before swine lest they be trampled upon. Because truth could be misunderstood, every attempt was made to keep it from those who might misuse it.

You may wonder whether it is possible to misapply truth or to use it destructively, and that of course would depend upon what truth you are thinking about and the truth about what. For example, today the area of learning related to the realm of the mind is almost completely untapped. No one up to the present time has undertaken a study of the mind from a correct standpoint even though thousands of years ago the secret of the mind was known in its fullness.

With the complete knowledge of mind and its operation in those early days came the abuse and misuse of such knowledge. Separate and apart from the ancient schools of wisdom, other schools which were called black brotherhoods, sprang up. In these brotherhoods, the membership consisted of some of the students who had received their original training in the wisdom schools and who perverted their knowledge to evil purposes and sometimes used it merely for personal or selfish ends; but whatever the purpose, the knowledge was used erroneously.

Out of that, in all the primitive races, there sprang up practices in which the mind was used for both good and evil. These practices have survived to this day among some kahunas in Hawaii and some of the natives in Australia, Central America, and in some parts of South America where those men of innate integrity use their powers for good—even for healing work —whereas those who have learned about the principles of mind and have not developed a sufficient degree of integrity have perverted the activity of mind and used it to further their own selfish interests. Such a perversion of truth-knowledge clearly shows that if truth falls into the wrong hands, it can wreak havoc with the lives of those who do not understand the truth that makes free. Today even in our civilized world, there are teachings which claim to be able to instruct students how to use the mind for purposes of good as well as for purposes of evil, that is, how to use the mind to influence people so that a person can get whatever he wants from them.

SYMBOLISM OF THE BIRTH OF JESUS

In the accounts of the birth of Jesus in the Gospels, the knowing student discerns the symbolic teaching of the ancients in which is is pointed out that simultaneously with the birth of the Christ enemies are roused up against It. And so the

Babe is taken into Egypt and hidden where those who would destroy It cannot find It. The Child is not returned until It is sufficiently advanced to be able to survive on Its own, or perhaps to outlive Its enemies.

Whenever a truth is announced to the world, enemies appear who are eager to destroy it. Those who are not ready for the spiritual experience unconsciously resent its attainment in anyone else and often instinctively rise up against it. That is why Paul said that the human mind is enmity against God. There are those who the moment they come anywhere near the Christ-spirit begin to fight It and everything that It represents. Wherever there is not a readiness for a spiritual way of life, spirituality breeds antagonism among the uninitiated and, when such people come into the presence of a spiritually illumined person, immediately the worst is aroused in them, and they fight anything or any person that seems to have a tiny grain of truth.

The Master revealed all this when he taught, "If they have persecuted me, they will also persecute you,"[1] and while he did not go on and point to others who had been persecuted before he came, he did reveal that wherever truth raises its head there will be enemies to destroy it, and often the enemy is of one's own household.

When we begin to look deeper and to penetrate the symbology of the birth of the Christ, we discover that it symbolizes the birth of truth within individual consciousness. Our mind is the manger in which the Christ is born. The enemies that would destroy it—the Herods and Caesars—are qualities of our own being, characteristics of our racial, religious, and nationalistic heritage which have become embedded and embodied within our minds, so that it is within our own minds that we find the enemy of the Christ.

All truth-teaching has to do with individual you and me, and consequently it is individual. Therefore, when it is re-

[1] John 15:20.

vealed that at a certain point in our development the Christ is born, it means that the Christ is born in us.

When it is revealed that an enemy of that Christ will rise up, it is well for us to remember that the enemy that will rise up is a quality or activity of our own human selves—something within ourselves; and when it is taught that the Christ must be taken into Egypt to be hidden, this means that truth must be practiced within us secretly, sacredly, and silently until it has had time to come to fruition, to come to the fullness of strength within us.

THE ENEMIES OF TRUTH IN HUMAN CONSCIOUSNESS

The greatest enemy of truth that exists within any individual is personal sense—that false sense of "I" which wants to be catered to or which seeks to use truth for personal or selfish motives. That is our greatest enemy.

As we study the life of the Master, we can see how completely and how frequently he acknowledged, "I can of mine own self do nothing.[2] . . . The Father that dwelleth in me, he doeth the works."[3] He always disclaimed personal credit, personal honor, and personal glory. His life was a dedication to the people of his own spiritual household, the people of his nation, race, and religion, and to all those receptive to his message.

In the end, he not only gave his life, but taught, "He that findeth his life shall lose it: and he that loseth his life for my sake shall find it."[4] Here, of course, he was not referring to any need of our being crucified on a cross, but rather to our losing our lives in the sense of not using truth for personal profit or personal fame, giving up any desire for personal adulation and personal gain, and thereby living our lives for the world.

The false sense of "I" which selfishly uses truth for personal gain and the real *I* which is willing to lose its "life for my sake" are symbolized by the black and the white brotherhoods. The white brotherhoods consist of those of such integrity that

2 John 5:30.   3 John 14:10.   4 Matthew 10:39.

every bit of truth known to them is used for the welfare of mankind. No one who is a part of the white brotherhood would ever be guilty of prostituting truth by using it for his own selfish purpose.

The black brotherhoods are made up of those who, learning the principles of truth, are not equal to living their lives unselfishly in dedication to the people of their world, but who see the opportunity of using this knowledge for personal fame, name, or gain. There are teachings being offered to the world today which instruct their adherents in the art of using the principles of good for destructive and selfish purposes. And so again there is the enemy of truth in human consciousness, that which would destroy truth.

The history of the world proves that throughout all time those who have used truth unwisely, selfishly, greedily, and evilly have themselves come to a sad end because the works they do react upon themselves. This also is in accord with the principle of "whatsoever a man soweth, that shall he also reap. For he that soweth to his flesh shall of the flesh reap corruption; but he that soweth to the Spirit shall of the Spirit reap life everlasting."[5] What they do to others is done unto themselves.

Those who utilize the principles of truth for selfish or evil purposes are merely laying up a whole storehouse full of evil for themselves. The karmic law never fails: it always reacts upon the one who uses it for evil, just as it also reacts for good upon those who use it for good. In other words, those who sow to the Spirit do reap life everlasting.

The bread that we cast upon the waters is the bread that returns to us. If the bread that we cast upon the waters is the bread of truth, life, and love, that is the bread that comes back to bless us; whereas, if we have sent forth corrupt bread— the bread of personalization, selfishness, greed, evil—that is the poisoned bread that returns to us.

[5] Galatians 6:7, 8.

LET THE WORLD WITNESS TRUTH THROUGH DEMONSTRATION

So we find in the symbology of truth the principles underlying truth. As we come to the Christmas season, let us remember, first of all, that we have been entrusted with a pearl
of wisdom, but because there is always an enemy ready to
destroy that pearl, let us learn to keep the gems of wisdom
secret and sacred within ourselves until such time as they have
come alive in us to such an extent that they are demonstrable,
and then the world can witness these principles in our experience without our having to talk about them or without our
having to boast about our knowledge.

In The Infinite Way, we have learned that it is no part of
our function to proselyte or to go out into the world in an
attempt to reform or save it. Our function is to abide within
ourselves, living the truth that has been revealed to us, and
then imparting and sharing whatever grain of truth we have
with those who seek us out. What we are, what we know, and
what we embody in our consciousness is so obvious that we
never need tell it to anyone: those within our orbit see and
feel it in us; they are drawn to us and eventually find their way
to us; and when they do, then is the time to share with them
whatever truth has come to us in demonstrable degree.

Never try to teach a truth that you yourself have not demonstrated at least in some measure, because that is to be asked
for bread and to give a stone. Never attempt to give out that
which you yourself have not assimilated and in some degree
can prove. You must be able to prove in some measure the
truth you voice, and it is the better part of wisdom to keep it
locked up inside of you, to practice it, and to live it, until you
have made it your own to such an extent that it is demonstrable,
and then it can be shared with those who come to you.

In The Infinite Way, we have been given principles of truth
not yet known to the world, and because there is not a sufficient
receptivity to them and a preparedness for them, it is not pos-

sible to give them to the world. But this does not mean that we cannot live and prove them in our individual experience, and then prove them for those who are led to us and, thereby, ultimately make them available to the world.

Never forget that the truth the Master Christ Jesus knew would have saved the world had the world been able to receive it. He said, "O Jerusalem, Jerusalem, thou that killest the prophets, and stonest them which are sent unto thee, how often would I have gathered thy children together, even as a hen gathereth her chickens under her wings, and ye would not!"[6] In other words, they could not receive what he had to offer. Gladly would he have given to the hierarchy of the Hebrew church all the wisdom that he had, but they could not receive it. Gladly, as he walked up and down the Holy Land, would he have taken all the people of his world under his arm, if they could have accepted him, but they would not.

And so it is that the world could never accept the truth that we have, and this truth would receive the same fate today that it received two thousand years ago if an attempt were made to send it abroad in the world with much fanfare. On the other hand, by publishing it, as we are doing, without advertising or promotion, it stands not only in your individual consciousness and mine, but it stands on the bookshelves of most of the seminaries and public libraries throughout the world. It stands there and day by day is being accepted by those individuals who are led to the shelves on which these books are to be found.

It is our function to celebrate Christmas by acknowledging the birth of the Christ in our consciousness and then hiding It there. Take your trip into Egypt, hide your Christ and let It grow, and then as It finds Its full strength and becomes demonstrable, slowly, gradually, gently, give It to those who seek you.

[6] Matthew 23:37.

FAILURE OF PRAYERS THAT SEEK A GOD-POWER

You will succeed in this work only in proportion as you understand and eventually demonstrate the principle of non-power which is a major principle of our work. Ever since the days of the pagans, attempts have been made to find and utilize a God-power. Turning to some supernatural power in the form of gods many to find a power to do what physical and mental powers could not accomplish was the origin of the pagan religions. And then came the monotheistic teaching of the Hebrews, but it also failed because, while it had one God, it sought to gain from that God the same power that the pagans had sought from their pagan gods.

There is no record, however, anywhere in Hebrew history of this God-power accomplishing for them what their prayers demanded except in the cases of individual Hebrew leaders like Moses, Elijah, Elisha, Isaiah, Jesus, John, and Paul, who were able to bring harmony, safety, and peace into the lives of their followers. But remember, these men did not pray as the other Hebrews prayed. Their prayers were fruitful because they had attained mystical wisdom and an understanding of true prayer. Throughout the centuries, the things the Hebrews sought of their God they never received except in those few intervals when their leaders were endowed with mystical wisdom.

The Christians have failed equally in their prayers, for they have been of as little avail as the old Hebrew prayers. In all the centuries of Christian prayer, there has been no end to war on earth, to plagues, storms, or to anything else that the Christians have prayed to have removed from their experience, including disease. Yet there have been some Christian mystics whose prayers have attained divine harmony, but, as in the case of the Hebrew mystics, only a few.

It is needless to call attention to the wars in which men have so fervently prayed for peace, and never once has that peace come except when the enemy had no more ammunition. Furthermore, the centuries of praying for health have been of no avail. Whatever advances have come in health have come not because of effective prayers, but because of the greater effectiveness of *materia medica*. The one exception to that rule is found among metaphysicians who have attained some measure of understanding of the nature of prayer.

Prayers that seek a God-power must fail. The very nature of God makes that inevitable. The nature of God is such that God cannot do one day what God is not doing every day, for God is the same yesterday, today, and forever. The nature of God is such that God could never do for one person what God is not doing for all people, for God cannot be a respecter of persons and still be God. God cannot be influenced by man. What kind of Omnipotence and Omniscience is God if man with his picayune knowledge can set himself up to advise God, tell or influence Him? God cannot be moved to change His laws or to make exceptions. His rain falls alike on the just and the unjust.

Trying to invoke God-power as the pagans and ancient Hebrews did, and as some Christians and Hebrews of today still do, must forever result in failure in much the same way as the scientists before Marconi's day failed when they were trying to find a power with which to overcome the nonexistent resistance in the air. Only when Marconi recognized the secret of nonpower did he succeed.

APPLYING THE PRINCIPLE OF NONPOWER

The powers of this world—the negative powers of sin, disease, unhappiness, the lack of supply or peace—these are not powers, and they operate as powers only as long as we individually, and the world collectively, can be made to fight them—to argue against them or to seek a power to destroy them. The way to harmony, whether in health, business, profession, art, or in human relationships is not found by invoking a God-power, because this God-power already is omnipresence, omnipotence, omniscience. It is already active where we are.

"The place whereon thou standest is holy ground"[7] because the presence of God is already there. If we make our bed in hell or if we walk through the valley of the shadow of death, we need not fear, for the very presence of God which we would invoke is already where we are. Omnipresence, Omnipotence, and Omniscience are our assurance that that which we are seeking, that which we are trying to contact, that which we are believing that we can gain even by sacrifice is already where we are —Omnipresence within our very being, within our own consciousness. The Christ is already born within us and is only awaiting our recognition.

Once we have given up the desire for a power which can be used, we shall have come into an awareness of the revelation which has been given us in this message and we shall learn the secret of "resist not evil."[8] Why did Jesus teach us to "resist not evil"? Why did he rebuke his disciples when they came to him and said, "Even the devils are subject unto us through thy name."[9] Because this was not truth: it was not true then and it is not true now that evil is subject to anyone by the name or the power of God. Jesus did not tell the impotent and the crippled man that the power of God would restore him, but rather, "Take up thy bed, and walk."[10] And there is the principle, a principle of life that cannot be used for selfish purposes to gain fame or fortune. It cannot be used for any personal means because this truth is neither on the level of matter or of mind, and therefore it is above and beyond the pairs of opposites.

Anything of a material or mental nature can be used for either good or evil. The same drug that is used to cure can be used to kill. Electricity, with all its convenient gadgets, can be a blessing, but it can also be destructive. Good food can build a

[7] Exodus 3:5.
[8] Matthew 5:39.
[9] Luke 10:17.
[10] John 5:8.

healthy body, but an excess of it can destroy one. Anything of a material or mental nature can be used for either good or evil.

It is only when we touch the realm of nonpower that we come into a realm where there is Something which cannot be used either for good or for evil, but which reveals Itself as good. We are not using It: It is enforcing Itself. For example, when the Master stated, "I can of mine own self do nothing," he revealed the principle which is basic to Infinite Way treatment. If we were to give anyone a treatment, it would be a mental activity, and that mental activity, as has been proved, can be used for good or for evil.

When we help our students and our patients, we do not give them treatments. We sit in the silence in the assurance of the nonpower of that which is appearing to afflict them; and therefore, no treatment, no mental application, and no mental projection of thought are necessary for we are simply sitting and beholding the nonpower. We are not utilizing one power over another—we are not even utilizing God-power because we are recognizing nonpower, the nonpower of that which is called the negative forces and influences of this world.

This principle of The Infinite Way is a radical departure from every other religious teaching in the world today. There is not one of which I have any knowledge that is using this particular principle. There are only vague hints of it in the four Gospels, and what may be discovered in other manuscripts we still do not know, but this that constitutes the major principle of The Infinite Way did not come to me through books, but through revelation, and it has been proved throughout thirty years of demonstration.

Our only value to this world will be in proportion to our ability to prove these principles first in our individual lives, then in the harmonies that take place within our families, and finally, in the degree of harmony, health, and peace that we can bring to those who are led to us, thereby eventually encompassing the globe and all the peoples of the world.

No student is called upon to go beyond his depth and if, in his individual experience, he is not able to understand and demonstrate this principle sufficiently to bring about the fulfillment of harmony in his own life, he has the right and the privilege to turn to other students for help and thereby to attain his own harmony, so that he can be free to carry on his studies and practice until he, too, is able to sit back when asked for help and, because of his understanding of the nature of that which is appearing as evil influences—as the sins or the diseases or the lacks or limitations of those who come to him—refrain from attempting to use any power.

Those who have been students of this work for a number of years are already working on the broader aspects of this principle as applied to the great world problems, and they are meeting with a measure of success. This work will continue until by its own demonstration it shows itself forth to the world.

ATTAIN THE CONSCIOUSNESS OF THE PRINCIPLE

Meanwhile, your responsibility first of all is, as was the case with Joseph and Mary, to take your Christ into Egypt and hide It within yourself. Continue to study and to practice and to live with these principles until they show themselves forth in your life to such an extent that others come to you and say, "What have you? What is it? Will you share it with me?" And then begin to feed them milk and gradually lead them to the meat of the Word.

In the beginning of your study and practice, you may believe that this is very simple. It appears much more simple than it is, and you will have many disappointments because it will seem so simple and logical as you read it that you will wonder why you cannot immediately demonstrate it, but you cannot demonstrate it merely because it is true. You can demonstrate it only in proportion as you attain the consciousness of it.

It is like mathematics. Mathematics is wholly true, but it does not always seem to do us much good when it comes to balancing our checkbooks, because sometimes we do not seem to have a thorough enough grasp of its principles. In other words, the mere fact that the principles of mathematics are true does not make them demonstrable for us. There has to be something further than the truth of mathematics: there has to be an *awareness* of the truth of mathematics, and then it will work.

So it is with this principle. Just because this principle is the principle of life does not mean that you can immediately apply it successfully. It takes time to develop the consciousness. There again we have the two years in Egypt and the example of St. Paul. Do you remember that after his many years of religious study Saul of Tarsus had a tremendous experience which came in the form of a blinding light in which he realized the Christ? You might expect that after such an experience he would start reforming the world the very next day—healing and doing mighty works. But instead of that, he went to Arabia for nine years and remained there all alone, pondering that which had been revealed to him, thinking of it, living it, and practicing it. Only after nine years did he begin his work.

In my own experience, a revelation was given to me late in 1928, but it was sixteen years after that before I began to teach, and those sixteen years were spent in proving in daily experience that these principles are true. This work is just like any art or science. The mere knowledge of it is not sufficient. There must be an actual consciousness behind the knowledge. That is why it takes time and patience and that is why we often have to resort to help from our fellow students until we reach that stage where we can walk on the water alone.

Let us rejoice, even though we are not able to walk on the water alone, that this great principle of nonpower has been given to us.

For unto us a child is born, unto us a son is given: and the government shall be upon his shoulder: and his name shall be called Wonderful, Counsellor, The mighty God, The everlasting Father, The Prince of Peace.

Arise, shine; for thy light is come, and the glory of the Lord
is risen upon thee.   ISAIAH 9:6; 60:1

ACROSS THE DESK

We know now that the Hebraic religion of old discovered
the ancient teaching of karmic law and thought that it was
God. All the teaching based on the Ten Commandments is
actually karmic law, and this explains why most of the Hebraic
prayers have remained unanswered.

Christ Jesus revealed God, the true God, and during his
ministry, he taught the nature of God and the way of prayer
with signs following, but when the Christian church was
founded, it completely dropped the God revealed by the Master
and substituted for its God the God of the Hebrews—karmic
law. The prayer of Hebrews and Christians alike is really a
petition that karmic law violate itself, and because that is an
impossibility, prayer remains unanswered.

Karmic law is the law of cause and effect, and wherever
there is cause there must be effect. The nature of cause must be
expressed as effect because cause and effect are inseparable and
indivisible. To reach the realm of God, it is necessary in consciousness to reach beyond the law into Grace—beyond cause
and effect into the consciousness which is above and beyond
cause and effect.

While we are in bondage to karmic law, we have no part in
God, nor does the activity of God function our lives. Karmic
law is not only revealed in the Ten Commandments, but likewise in such well-known passages as "whatsoever a man soweth,
that shall he also reap. For he that soweth to his flesh shall
of the flesh reap corruption; but he that soweth to the Spirit
shall of the Spirit reap life everlasting.[11] . . . Therefore all
things whatsoever ye would that men should do to you, do ye
even so to them: for this is the law and the prophets."[12]

Paul reveals that the creature, that is, he who lives in the

[11] Galatians 6:7, 8.   [12] Matthew 7:12.

realm of cause and effect, is not under the law of God, neither indeed can be. "But ye are not in the flesh, but in the Spirit, if so be that the Spirit of God dwell in you. . . . For as many as are led by the Spirit of God, they are the sons of God"[13]— under His law, care, and supply.

When the Master taught that "My kingdom is not of this world.[14] . . . My peace I give unto you: not as the world giveth, give I unto you,"[15] he revealed that such a God is above and beyond "this world"—the world of cause and effect. And in the Sermon on the Mount, he revealed the nature of the Son of God as living above the law and as living by Grace.

The era in which we are now living is witnessing the breaking up of the evils of "this world." Causes set in motion by the mind of man—separate and apart from any God-contact—have given us the evils of slavery and of national domination and exploitation. They brought to the world the evils of tyranny, of ecclesiastical power, of nineteenth- and twentieth-century capitalism, and of commercial and religious wars.

The mid-twentieth century is witnessing the breaking up of these evils and the introduction of the state of consciousness which is revealed in the command to "love thy neighbour as thyself."[16] There will soon be ushered in an age, now already somewhat in evidence, which will reveal man living at peace and in harmony with his neighbors, near and far. There will be no enmity manifest on earth, and very little hidden malice. Human love will be expressed at every level of life and in countless ways. This will be a long period of peace on earth and good will among men.

During this time, those instructed in the spiritual kingdom, those who have attained God-awareness, those who have risen above even the good in the law of cause and effect will be preparing the way for the final experience—the kingdom of God on earth.

[13] Romans 8:9, 14.
[14] John 18:36.
[15] John 14:27.
[16] Matthew 19:19.

The evidence of the kingdom of God on earth will be the attainment of God-consciousness, and thereby God-government by individuals and small groups. This consciousness will penetrate and permeate human consciousness more easily after the grosser elements of human sense have been eliminated, and all human consciousness will be raised "until he come whose right it is"[17]—until His reign is established on earth.

During the period of the Christmas celebrations, remember, just once in a while, that the events you are celebrating appeared first as only the planting of seeds, seeds from which rich fruitage is now appearing on earth. As you first enter the spiritual path, you seek only to solve your own problems or the problems of those nearest and dearest to you. Later, perceiving the nature of spiritual work, you *die* to yourself and understand that you are discovering universal Truth, and by bearing witness to Its grace, you are planting the seeds for future generations, the fruitage of which will be world peace, joy, and divine sonship.

[17] Ezekiel 21:27.

Index

In each entry the number before the colon indicates the page, the number following the colon indicates the paragraph on that page.

181